THE
ROMEO
AND JULIET
DELUSION

FINDING FREEDOM AFTER TRAUMA

A MEMOIR

LORI ABBOTT

Lori Abbott
Fargo, ND
ljabbott15@gmail.com
www.loriabbott.pubsitepro.com
www.Facebook.com/lorijabbott/

Limits of Liability and Disclaimer of Warranty
The author and publisher shall not be liable for your misuse of this material. This book is strictly for informational and educational purposes.

Warning – Disclaimer
Names and identifying details have been changed to protect privacy. The author is not a physician, psychologist, or qualified expert on addiction or trauma recovery. All of the content in this book is for informational purposes only. It is not intended to be a substitute for medical advice, diagnosis or treatment from any mental health or addiction issue. Readers should consult a medical, health, or competent professional before adopting any of the suggestions in this book or drawing inferences from it. The purpose of this book is to educate and entertain. The author and/or publisher do not guarantee that anyone following these techniques, suggestions, tips, ideas, or strategies will become successful. The author and/or publisher shall have neither liability nor responsibility to anyone with respect to any loss or damage caused, or alleged to be caused, directly or indirectly by the information contained in this book.

GET YOUR FREE GIFT!

A FREE CHECKLIST

I have created a free checklist to help you determine if you or someone you love is in an unhealthy/abusive relationship.

- Checklists serve as a powerful tool to identify concerning behaviors and safety risks.
- Checklists provide you with a way to acknowledge and assess unhealthy aspects of your relationship.
- Checklists are private and confidential.

Go to **www.loriabbott.pubsitepro.com** to pick up your free gift and to find out about my upcoming events!

Please email me with any questions or comments regarding *The Romeo & Juliet Delusion* at **ljabbott15@gmail.com**.

ACKNOWLEDGMENT

Thank you to Maicy Mai. The most beautiful soul that I have been blessed to connect with. I would not be who I am today without your love, light, and energy. We live an extraordinary life together, hand in paw.

*This book is dedicated to my
daughter in heaven, Brea.*

*Brea danced above my soul. Guiding me to
put my thoughts into words, words into pages,
pages into a book, and a book out into the
Universe. With brave wings we fly together.*

Lori Abbott is a lawyer with over 15 years of experience in the areas of family and criminal law. She holds a BA in criminal justice and social welfare from Mankato State University and a JD from William Mitchell College of Law.

Throughout the course of her career, Abbott has dedicated countless hours of free legal representation to women seeking domestic abuse protection orders. She also spent many years in private practice volunteering at a Rape and Abuse Crisis Center, where she saw firsthand the effects of abuse and trauma on women and children every day.

After a near-death experience at the hands of her former fiancé in 2015, she found herself in the same exact shoes of all those women she spent her life professionally representing.

In *The Romeo & Juliet Delusion*, Abbott brings a unique perspective to the subject matter as a successful family and criminal law attorney. Her story shows that addiction and the possibility of drowning in a toxic relationship can happen to anyone. Through the retelling of her own abuse at the hands of someone she deeply loved, readers can understand that domestic violence and addiction do not care about race, gender, job title, or educational level.

Abbott offers an inspiring vision of what is possible for victims on the other side of trauma, abuse, and addiction—all while revealing how she overcame her own personal battles that so strongly parallel the women she serves and the countless number of women around the world currently trapped in this dangerous type of relationship.

Much like the clients she serves, Abbott was forced to embark upon the greatest challenge of her life: learning to heal from her own trauma, abuse, and addictions. Throughout this journey, she was called upon by the Universe to fully own her story and share it with the world. In addition to the writing of this book, she has started going public with her story by being a guest speaker on live Facebook interviews, morning radio shows in her local community, podcasts, and various in-person speaking engagements.

Abbott is an avid world traveler, life adventurer, and an extreme sports enthusiast. She currently resides in Fargo, North Dakota, with her dog, Maicy. In addition to practicing law, Abbott is a volunteer Wish Granter with Make-A-Wish, a literacy coach at a non-profit Dyslexia Learning Center, and a youth mentor for underprivileged girls through the YMCA.

CONTENTS

I awoke to a doctor standing over me in the hospital room, telling me that I needed to wake up. There were police officers who needed to talk to me. I kept my eyes tightly closed thinking if I did that long enough, everyone would leave.

Eventually, though, I had to talk to them. I couldn't form thoughts. I felt sick, confused, and completely overwhelmed. As I went over in my mind the facts of what had happened over the past 48 hours, tears poured down my face, and the police started asking me so many questions.

"Where is he?" they asked.

"I don't know," I replied.

"When did you last have contact with him?"

"I don't know."

"Did he force you to do something you did not want to do?"

"I don't know."

It was the only answer I had in me for the next 20 questions that came my way.

The Romeo & Juliet Delusion is an inspirational memoir about the dangerous relationship with my former fiancé, who was a meth and heroin addict. In addition to the overwhelming aspects of being the significant other of a drug addict, there was physical and emotional abuse, including some very traumatic events that happened over the course of our long-term relationship that escalated to a near-death experience in 2015.

I am sharing my story to provide readers with a better understanding of two of the most serious social crises in the world today: drug addiction and domestic violence. From both the perspective of my personal experiences as well as from the perspective of being a family and criminal law attorney for over 15 years, I am providing a rare and unique insight into the reality of deeply loving a drug addict, remaining in a dangerous relationship for much too long, and watching my life deteriorate as I was desperately trying to save his life.

The World Health Organization (WHO) reports that one in three women worldwide will be subjected to partner violence in their lifetime. The National Center for Health Statistics (NCHC) reports there are 253 drug abuse deaths every single day. As the reader journeys with me through both my dark days and my light days, they will learn to acknowledge their own addictions, toxic relationships, and unhealed traumas. I share a self-help modality of approaching addiction and domestic violence from the perspective of curiosity and compassion rather than judgment and criticism. These particular life experiences are shameful, and people in similar circumstances crave a relatable writer and an authentic path to healing from someone who blazed the trail herself with blood, tears, and endless mistakes.

After my relationship ended, I spent the next six years of my life experimenting with different ways to free my soul from the traumas I experienced. I initially thought the solution to healing was to simply close the door on the entire experience, but what I learned along the way was that this was not going to be a situation where the experience could just be locked away nor a return to a "normal" life as if it had never happened at all. Rather, it was going to be a situation that required me to reincarnate myself and use my insight and experiences to help other people do the same. Being a victim of your circumstances is not where life ends, but rather where life can truly begin again.

As a successful professional woman, I never could have imagined ending up in the relationship I did or living the life I led. Do not ever think something cannot happen to you. Life has a very strange way of proving us wrong.

CHAPTER 1

FATAL ATTRACTION

I often look back and wonder who I really was the night I met Romeo. It was definitely the calm before the blackest, most dangerous storm of my life. I had just recently walked away from a successful 15-year career of being a family and criminal trial attorney in Minneapolis, Minnesota, to pursue a non-traditional legal career path. Initially, it was like a whole new world had opened before me. I took a position doing due diligence research for a company that allowed me to work from home. I was working eight-hour days with the ability to set my schedule, rather than being confined to an office working 14-hour days. I found myself with more free time than I had ever had in my adult life. However, I soon began to miss the adrenaline rush of trial work and fell into a mundane routine of work, going to the gym, and hanging out with the few friends that I had in my life that were not busy raising families. An ordinary person would have thought it was the perfect life. But I was bored, lonely, and unfulfilled. I was born with a wild and restless soul that I was able to keep controlled with a high-pressure, all-consuming career.

I was almost 40 years old and had reluctantly accepted the reality that after having a stillborn baby many years ago, I was not going to be able to conceive another baby. There were complications from my labor and delivery that stole from me the opportunity I wanted most: to be a mom. This left me with a void that was crying in desperation to be filled with something or someone. I had achieved more career success than I ever had thought possible, and despite the loss of my baby girl and subsequent divorce, I had lived an amazing life full of excitement, adventure, travel, and true periods of happiness and peace. But quitting trial work changed me, and my soul desperately needed more out of life than what I was currently experiencing. I was exhausted from the responsibility that I had carried my entire life since childhood and sought freedom from everything that had kept me boxed into a conformed way of living. I was in a state of discontent and unrest with every single aspect of my life. I had been dating a guy for a couple of months, but I knew the relationship was going nowhere. I had been preparing to break it off, but just had not gotten around to actually doing it by the time Romeo first entered my life.

To this day, I still get butterflies in my stomach as I remember the night our eyes and souls first met. It was a warm fall night. Chad, my boyfriend at the time, and I decided to take his Harley over to Neumann's Bar in St. Paul for Bike Night. The inside of the bar was packed, so we walked out back, where there was an outdoor patio bar. There was Romeo, quietly drinking a bottle of Coors Light by himself at the bar. I remember exactly what he was wearing down to his baby blue T-shirt and the exact type of shoes. He looked up at me, and I looked at him from across the bar. The attraction was overwhelming. It was electrifying and literally took my breath away. I had never come close to ever experiencing anything like that in my entire life. It simply could not be real. How is it possible for someone to actually have this kind of instant connection to another person by merely looking at each other across a crowded room? Isn't this just supposed to happen in a romance movie?

Chad and I walked up to the bar and ordered beers. He instantly started up a random conversation with Romeo while I just sat there taking in his presence, his voice, his mannerisms, and those wild, intoxicating brown eyes. I was drawn to everything about him. I learned that Romeo worked in the same field as Chad—construction—and they both loved Harley Davidson motorcycles. We soon discovered that Romeo was waiting for his girlfriend, who was driving in from out of town. When he found out that I was a family law attorney, he asked me a few questions about Brynlee, his youngest daughter's child support case. I was tongue-tied, my heart was beating out of my chest, and I just remember looking into those eyes and feeling alive—and a little like I just wanted to jump in his lap at the bar. I found myself fantasizing about him taking my hand and leading me out of the bar and onto the back of his motorcycle. And I believed that he felt the exact same way. It was intoxicating.

Romeo's girlfriend soon showed up, and the four of us had drinks and enjoyed the live music. At the end of the night, Chad and Romeo exchanged phone numbers so that they could connect about an upcoming job they planned on working together. Romeo asked if I had a card so he could give me a call to discuss Brynlee's child support case in more detail. I handed him my card, which he carefully tucked away in his wallet. I went home that night, with only him on my mind. For the next several weeks, the four of us double-dated a couple of times. It was awkward going on a double date when there was such a strong gravitational pull to being with someone other than the person you were with. Neither Romeo nor I wanted to be dating the people we were with, even though we never discussed this until later. I soon thereafter ended things with Chad, and both he and Romeo became only a memory. But for weeks, not a day went by that I did not think about Romeo and how I felt when I was around him.

About two months later, I received a call from him on a Sunday night. He started asking me a few questions about his child support case and then asked me if I was still seeing Chad, and I said no. He told me that did not surprise him and that he knew Chad was not right for me. I asked if he was still seeing Michelle, and he said no. He then asked me if I had ever thought about him, and I told him every single day, and he shared that it was the same for him. He asked if I would like to go on a date with him. He had not even finished getting the words out of his mouth before I screamed yes into the phone.

Romeo was living about 90 miles south of where I was, in Albert Lea, Minnesota, so we made plans for Thursday of that week. He would be coming to Minneapolis to see me, and we would figure out the details over the next couple of days. My body was on fire as I hung up the phone. I literally danced around my home as the thought of seeing him caused the adrenaline to pulse through my entire body. His voice alone made me tremble. He called two days later, and I told him that I was able to get tickets to the Vikings football game. He was so excited. We made plans to meet at a bar just outside of downtown for a beer and early dinner and then head to the 7:00 p.m. game. He asked if he should get a hotel room, and I told him that I had connections to a hotel downtown and could get him a room at no charge. I obviously knew, just as he did, that I would be sharing that room with him.

When Thursday finally arrived, I was like a 5-year-old child on Christmas morning. I was overwhelmed with excitement to see him. The day endlessly dragged by. My co-workers kept asking me why I could not sit still and what in the hell was wrong with me. I told them I had a date. I called my best friend several times that day rambling on about how excited I was. No one had ever seen me like that before. I had never seen myself like that before. After watching the clock slowly tick by all day long, it was finally time to go meet Romeo. I got to the bar a little while before he did, sat down, and ordered a beer. My stomach was in knots.

Then he walked through the door. Everything about him was as perfect as the memories that had carved themselves into my mind. His perfectly groomed hair, those eyes that held mystery, all of his tattoos, his tanned, muscular arms, his Rock Revival jeans, and his Affliction shirt. Our biker chic clothing styles matched, and everything about his appearance was attractive to me. The way he carried himself as he walked, the way he smelled, the way he said, "Hello, beautiful," as he sat down next to me. We just stared at each other in silence. The chemistry between us was palpable. Romeo's gentle touch on my leg or arm radiated electricity through my entire body. We had two drinks and dinner. I told him I would drive downtown, so we left his truck in the parking lot of the bar.

We had so much fun at the game and later joked that neither of us could remember the score or any big plays because we were too enthralled with sitting next to each other. Romeo took my hand and kissed it, telling me how long overdue this was for us to be alone. He loved professional sports as much as I did, and he had never been to a Vikings game before, so it was special that it was our first date. Oddly enough, his parents were also in from out of town and attending the game. I actually met them during halftime. It was strange to meet the parents of a man you were on your first official date with, but considering they rarely attended games, it was good timing. I learned that Romeo was very close to his mother—something I deeply admired in a man. He explained that his mom was the only person that he could count on and that he owed her a lot for all the hell had put her through over the years.

The colors and sounds of a Thursday night in downtown Minneapolis seemed so much more vibrant and exciting with Romeo's arm around my waist or his fingers tickling the small of my back. I had never felt so much chemistry with anyone. I had waited months to be able to spend time alone with him. After the game, we walked to a nearby bar for a drink before making our way to the hotel. There was fire between us. As soon as we stepped into the elevator of the hotel, he finally kissed me. I was overcome with emotion as he hugged me tight. As we lay down in bed next to each other, I knew every fantasy of what had played over and over in my head for the past couple of months was about to happen for real. I wanted to have sex with Romeo that night more than anything, but I had never slept with anyone on the first date, so I waited until the following morning to ease my guilt—as if that made any difference. It was fucking amazing, even hotter than all the fantasies I had created in my mind when I was alone.

He told me to call in sick to work, saying he had just finished a big concrete job and did not have anywhere he needed to be. So, for the first time in my entire life, I called in sick to work. It was Friday and I had already gotten most of my hours for the week anyway, so why not? I did not want to leave Romeo and go back home to reality. I wanted to stay in the bubble of lust and excitement a little while longer. We went and had breakfast. He asked me if I had ever been to Nisswa, Minnesota, and I said no. He said, "Let's go on a road trip. I have a lake cabin about 10 miles outside of Nisswa."

So without considering how risky it was to leave town with him, off we went. When we got to the cabin, he whipped out a credit card from his wallet and opened the locked door with it. I stood there and asked, "Why didn't you use a key?"

He laughed and said, "I wasn't planning on coming here when I left home, so I don't have my key."

It seemed plausible. However, this was no typical guy's cabin that I had ever been in; it was a home. (I later found out it was his parent's year-round lake home, not his cabin, and that he never had a key because his stepfather would not allow him to have one.)

We spent the rest of the weekend driving around on back country roads, drinking beer, singing to the radio together, telling each other our life stories, and having wild sex several times a day. He told me that he had been in some trouble in his 20s and had ended up in prison for a short time. He also shared more details about being a recovered drug addict and how he wanted to get all that out in the open, but assured me that it was in his past and staying there. He was the father of two little girls now and had learned from his mistakes. I believed him. He also shared with me some deeply troubling and traumatic experiences that happened to him as a child. He said he had been physically and sexually abused by more than one person and had even been kidnapped as a young boy, but did not want to go into any more detail about those things. If anything, knowing all these things about him just added to his wild, bad-boy image that instantaneously and toxically attracted me to him.

On Saturday night of that weekend, we were off-roading in my Jeep, and a song came on the radio. It was "Cowboys and Angels," one of my favorite songs. Romeo stopped the vehicle, turned up the music, and we danced under the stars as he sang every word of the song to me, except where he improvised that he was "way wilder than a cowboy," and I improvised that I was "no fucking angel." It became one of our songs for years to come. To this day, it moves me to tears when I hear it. As wild and troubled as Romeo sincerely was, there was a soft, loving side of him that I may forever be the only person to have caught a fleeting glimpse of. He was the first person that I could just be myself with, and I deeply longed for that my entire life. There was no professional image or responsibility that I was obligated to hold up in his eyes. I was free for the first time in my life to just be who I truly was. That night, I was simply a girl who had fallen madly in love with a boy as we danced under the twinkling stars. Romeo asked if I could spend one more night with him, so I did. I just left my boss a message indicating that I still wasn't feeling better but would be back to my normal hours on Tuesday.

I finally returned back home from our first date five days later. Those first few days together are the happiest memories I have of any relationship that I have ever experienced in my life. The way Romeo held me so tightly through the night. The way my body felt when he simply touched it. The way his voice sounded when he spoke. His confidence, spontaneity, and fearless sense of adventure. My wild and restless soul finally being settled by another human being—something I had never dreamt was possible, let alone that quickly.

What I did not realize at the time was that I was already becoming addicted to Romeo—one of the many lessons I have learned the hard way about addiction. I went from stagnation to intoxicating, reckless abandonment in a dangerously short period of time. The dichotomy between those two existences was the greatest rush I had ever felt in my life, and I was hooked.

Romeo went back to Albert Lea and said he would call me when he got home, and we would figure out when we could see each other again. Beginning the next week, he started coming to Minneapolis almost every weekend. After just a few weeks, I met Brynlee. She was only 2 years old when Romeo and I started dating. We formed an instant bond, almost as intense as the bond that I felt toward Romeo. Brynlee was in need of a mother, and I was longing for a daughter. Her mom was having a hard time letting go of Romeo. She was more concerned about running wild and finding a new boyfriend than she was about mothering Brynlee. She would push her off on anyone who would take her so that she could have her freedom. Two weeks later, I met Romeo's older daughter, Emma (The girls had different mothers.). Romeo came to Minneapolis, and we went to Emma's school so he could surprise her with an unplanned visit. I watched as he waited outside the school for her to come out. She ran up to him and gave him a big hug. He swung her pink teddy bear backpack over one of his broad shoulders and took her hand as they walked down the street to our vehicle. She looked up at him as they held hands and laughed. I fell even more in love with Romeo in those moments watching him walk hand-in-hand with Emma. We took her for a burger and fries at Neumann's and explained to her that was where we had met each other. Emma looked at me the way only a 7-year-old could and asked, "Do you love my dad?" Romeo and I had not said those words yet. He instantly looked at Emma and said, "She better, because I love her almost as much as I love you."

The next time he came to town, he wanted me to meet his sister and brother-in-law, so we made plans to have dinner at their house. They were running a little late, so Romeo and I stopped for a beer at what had become one of our favorite bars. He could not sit still, and he was disconnected from me for the very first time. Something was really off. Usually he was very affectionate, always tracing my skin with his fingertips, holding my hand, or pulling my face into his for a kiss. But not today. He had hardly touched me. He also kept getting into screaming arguments with Brynlee's mother on the phone over simple things that should not have been confrontational. This was a very different side of Romeo than I had seen before, and it was unsettling to hear so much anger he had toward the mother of his child. I learned that day that she had taken out a domestic abuse restraining order against him. He told me she was a crazy liar and had severe addiction issues. Of course, I believed him. We were sitting at the bar, and he suddenly pulled out a tiny plastic bag from his pocket and placed it in my hand. I picked it up, looked at it; it was empty. I asked him what it was, and he just laughed, held my face in his hands, and kissed me, telling me how much he loved me.

I remembered that this was not the first time that Romeo had pulled out these empty little bags in front of me or laid them on the kitchen cupboard. I had also found them in the pockets of his jeans when I was doing laundry and in his truck. I also often found small, rolled-up squares of aluminum foil. I didn't really think anything about it at the time. Construction workers come home with shit in their pockets every day. What I learned was all of these little bags once contained the meth and heroin that Romeo was using every day that we were together. He finally calmed down after a couple of beers, and we ended up having a great evening at his sister's home.

Over the next month, Romeo increasingly became harder to get a hold of, and his stories about where he was and what jobs he was working often did not match up. I also was getting upset that he had not had me down to his house in Albert Lea. He always said he hated it there and would rather come to Minneapolis. It bothered me, but I let it go. He also reminded me every chance he could that he liked coming to Minneapolis because he also got to see Emma and wanted me to spend as much time as possible getting to know her. One night, I caught him in a complete lie over his whereabouts. He called to tell me that he was not going to be able to make it to Minneapolis that night because his job in Owatonna was taking longer than he thought. However, early in the day he texted me a picture of him working in a completely different town. I called him out on the lie, and he got very defensive and told me that I must have read the text wrong. I told him he was lying and that I needed a week to think about things.

Romeo called me the next morning and told me to come down to Albert Lea to see him on Friday night, so I did. I met him at a house where he claimed he lived with his roommate. I asked why Brynlee and Emma did not have any of their things there. It seemed like a college party house, not a home where a 35-year-old man lived and would have his young daughters stay at, and was nothing at all like "his" beautiful lake cabin. I could sense he was very uncomfortable in the house (later I found out he used to live there but didn't anymore because his roommate kicked him out) and kept urging me to pick a place to have dinner. I grew suspicious. I asked to see his Harley. He told me it was in storage for the winter and not there. I then asked where the sleds were, as he had been telling me since I met him about the two Arctic Cat snowmobiles he had and how excited he was for us to ride together. He got a strange look on his face and insisted that we needed to leave; he was ready for a beer and to have me meet a friend of his. I had yet to meet any of his friends, so I let all those suspicions fade away and compliantly did exactly what Romeo wanted to do—a dangerous pattern that became the norm in our relationship. At the end of the night, I was getting tired and told him I wanted to go back to his house and go to bed. He said we couldn't.

I asked, "What in the hell are you talking about?"

He said, "We need to go back to Minneapolis, babe, because I am feeling lucky and want to go to the casino."

I told him no. It was 1:00 a.m. We needed to pick up Brynlee later in the day, so it made no sense for us to drive so far to the casino and then back to Albert Lea to pick her up.

He just laughed and said, "Let's go, babe," so of course I did. Another pattern that became the norm in our relationship. Romeo told me what we were doing, and I did it. No questions asked. Romeo was constantly texting while he was driving and did not say a word to me. We got to the casino. He told me to wait in the vehicle and he would be right back. He was gone for over an hour. He did not answer his phone. I went in and searched the casino but could not find him anywhere. I was tired and angry, so I took a cab back to my house. He called a few minutes after I got home and said he was sorry, that he had run into an old friend and lost track of time. He came over, but could not sleep, so I finally told him to go lie on the couch and watch TV so that I could get some sleep.

The next morning, I got up and asked what time we were leaving for Albert Lea because I wanted to get my vehicle and we needed to pick up Brynlee. Romeo was acting very paranoid. He got up and started going through my bathroom drawers and my bedroom closet asking me if some other man had been in my apartment since the last time he was there. I told him he was acting crazy and that we needed to leave. We finally got on the road. He asked me for my phone, so I gave it to him. He started going through all my contacts and text messages and started drilling me with questions about who people were and why I had them in my phone. I grabbed my phone back. He suddenly started punching the dashboard of his truck, completely shattering the radio. He was wild and screaming incoherently at the top of his lungs. I began to cry and asked him what in the fuck was wrong with him. This was the first time that I was scared of Romeo. He eventually calmed down, and it was like watching someone first wake up in the morning after a very deep sleep. It was as if he did not even realize what he had just done. I believe in all honesty that he did not. He tried explaining to me that sometimes he literally sees the color red, and when that happens, everyone needs to get away from him because he has to scream and pound on something until the vision goes away. I did not understand, but I believed he was telling me the truth because he was embarrassed and very apologetic—two demeanors Romeo had never shown before.

Over the next two months, his inconsistent and bizarre behavior continued. Sometimes he was "normal," and we spent time as a family with his daughters, doing the things you imagine a couple would typically do. I started to really get to know his mom. She told me a lot of troubling things about Romeo—things that he had been less than honest about—such as, he had been in and out of treatment countless times and jail more times than she could count. He had also been suicidal many times, and she had lost years of her life worrying about whether or not he was ever going to straighten his life out. Every woman he had dated in the past had serious issues and were not good influences for an already troubled man. She said she was so grateful that he had met me, someone who had never been in trouble or involved in using drugs, and that he had finally decided to settle down and be a father to his daughters.

Romeo also became always short of money and continued to not be truthful with me about his whereabouts when we were not together. He would tell me one thing in the morning and something completely different when he called to say good night. One day, he told me that he was not going to make it to town because he had to take care of Brynlee, but I knew that Brynlee was with his mom because I had just talked to them on the phone. Other times, he was depressed and suicidal. He called late one night and told me he had a bad day, that he had a gun and did not want to live any longer. I asked where he was, and he told me on a gravel road somewhere between Albert Lea and Minneapolis. He claimed he did not know how he got there, but that he needed me to come help him.

I immediately got up and started driving toward Albert Lea. It took me hours to locate his whereabouts, but I eventually found him sitting in his truck. He looked disheveled; his eyes were dilated and wild. He had sweat pouring down his face, and his entire body was shaking. I searched the truck and could not find a gun. He said he threw it when he saw headlights because he knew the cops were after him. I asked him why the cops were after him, and he said, "for bad things I have done."

I finally got him to agree to get in my vehicle and come home with me. He got in the driver's seat and started driving. He suddenly stopped in the middle of the road. He grabbed my hand and looked deep into my eyes and said words that I will never forget: "You need to get the fuck away from me, and stay away from me. There is something wrong with me, and I am going to end up killing you."

That was the second time that I was scared of Romeo. The first time was when he flipped into a rage and shattered the radio in the vehicle, but I felt that was not about me. I was scared of his anger then, but now he had directed that anger and mental instability at me. However, I did not get away from him. I could not get away from him. I felt trapped. I did not know how to let go of him. I did not want to let go of him. I wanted to fix him. I believed that I could. But I learned the hard way that was not possible.

CHAPTER 2

BONNIE AND CLYDE

Romeo told me a few days later that he had ended up on that country road because he had a relapse with cocaine. He explained that someone on a job site had it, and before he could even think, he just did a few lines, but that he had only used a few times and was scared of where this would lead him. He told me how much he loved me and that he had already stopped, so I had nothing to worry about, and things would go back to how they were before.

Romeo and I were sitting at the table eating dinner later that week. He had been irritable and combative all day and buried in his phone. I felt unsettled and walked on eggshells around him, trying to avoid confrontation. He suddenly grabbed his keys and said he was going to run to get cigarettes and a Mountain Dew and would be right back. An hour went by. Five hours went by. Days went by. Throughout this time, he would send random text messages saying he was "handling something," and that is all I needed to know.

I called his mom, who genuinely seemed worried, but told me, "He does this sometimes." We discussed his relapse and our fear that this had not been just a few days of using cocaine. I started thinking back over all his behavior over the past few months, and I knew he had been using drugs, but I did not want to accept that and all the consequences I would need to face. All I cared about was finding him and getting him into treatment. Romeo had experienced short-lived success with remaining clean, but he had me this time and his daughters. He had also told me repeatedly that he would go to treatment if that meant I would stay by his side. I convinced myself that treatment would work this time. I also just needed the insanity to stop so that I could think.

Four days later, he called in the middle of the night. I started screaming, "Where in the fuck are you, and what in the fuck is going on?"

His breathing was labored, and he was manic. "I need you to come get me now, babe. You need to get me away from these people now before it is too late."

I asked him where he was, and he said the casino. I drove to the parking lot of the casino. It took him an hour to call me back, but he eventually came out and got in the vehicle. He was still wearing the same clothes he had left in almost a week earlier. He was dirty, smelled, was shaking uncontrollably, and kept flicking the door lock switch on and off and on and off. I started asking a hundred questions to which he responded, "I need you to just shut the fuck up and let me think."

I turned on the radio and he immediately leaned over, grabbed my arm, and screamed, "I told you I need everything to be quiet," and then proceeded to dent every inch of my dashboard with his fists and shatter my radio into a hundred pieces.

The rage inside of him utterly paralyzed me. We proceeded to drive home in silence. We walked into the house, and he told me to sit down on the couch. He closed all the blinds and taped a piece of paper over the peephole on the front door. He then proceeded to open all the bedroom doors, closets, and cupboards and then asked if there was anybody on the balcony. He was completely coming undone. I froze in fear. He continued to hysterically pace around the house for the next two hours and forced me to sit on the couch. I told him I needed to get ready for work, as I needed to go into the office that day rather than work remotely. He said he would drive me there and then come pick me up. I did not like the idea of him having my vehicle, but I was scared to tell him no. He called non-stop the entire time that I was at work. I finally just told him to come get me. He was still wearing the same clothes and had not showered but was calmer; he was exhausted.

When we got home, I looked at Romeo and said, "So this is what a relapse is like, huh?" He said he had used something other than cocaine and that he gotten some dirty shit that really fucked him up. I told him I was not going to live like this and that he either needed to get into treatment or he needed to go. He said he did not need treatment; he just needed to sleep it off for a few days. I did not push it further. He was home safe and needed sleep, and so did I.

I woke him up a couple of times over the next two days because I assumed he had homeowners to call about jobs since he had not been to work in a week. I could not get him to do anything or really even wake up completely. On the third day, he got up and we talked. He was soft and gentle as he began to inform me of who I had actually been dating this whole time.

Romeo said he was clean the night we met and all the time that we hung out together with our exes, but had relapsed on meth and heroin shortly after the last time he had seen me. He was high the night of the Vikings game and every day since. He said he was able to keep it from me because he was mixing all kinds of drugs that "balanced" him out so that he could sleep on the weekends and the nights that we were together. He admitted he did not have a house in Albert Lea and had actually been spending most nights he was not with me at various casinos or crashing on someone's couch. I asked him about work, and he said he had not worked a construction job in months because he had to pawn all his tools for dope. I asked where the money came from for the rest of the dope, the nights at the casino, the cash he had at times, his child support payments, etc. He had no straight answers but told me he was way behind in child support, so the County was after him. He also admitted that he had an open felony theft case because he had not been making restitution payments, so his probation had been revoked, and he would soon have a warrant out. Romeo then did what Romeo did best: con me into believing he was the victim of his past, that he loved me more than anything and would do anything to make things right again. Those brown eyes were back to being soft and intoxicating, but with more pain and darkness behind them than any one person should ever have. I looked at his arm and saw all the fresh track marks. I felt his remorse and shame. He told me so many times that he didn't want to be the way he was. I believed that he did not want that lifestyle and instead wanted a lifestyle of an intact family with me and his daughters. But, he needed professional help to become that person. He held me tight, and I forgave him. Yet another pattern that became the norm in our relationship.

The next month was better. Romeo started a new job working for a concrete company and was staying clean. Every time he left the house saying he was going to run errands, my stomach got knots in it, and I was constantly calling him, but he always was doing what he was supposed to be doing. I was starting to slowly rebuild just a little trust in him. However, this phase did not last long. About six weeks later, he started becoming very moody and restless; everything bored him, and he quit his job, indicating that co-workers were using drugs on the jobsite, and he could not stay clean around users. I asked him if he would consider at least finding a sponsor, to which he responded, "I do not need a sponsor. I only need you. You are the first good person I have ever dated and the only person who believes that there is good in me."

Both statements rang true. Romeo had never had a healthy, supportive, loving relationship. He had told me many times that he did not think that anyone would ever see the good in him and that my ability to do so was one of the reasons that he loved me so much. I asked him if he thought about getting high, and he said every single day, all day long.

I was in over my head in more ways than I knew. I found a Nar-Anon meeting (a support meeting for the family members of addicts) the next day and, unknown to Romeo, started going for a few weeks. I thought that it would help me to be in contact with other people in my situation. Unconsciously, I was really longing for someone to intervene and get me to the point of being able to safely leave him. That never happened. It was a very small meeting, and I felt the problems the other people shared were not even close to the serious issues I was dealing with, so I did not feel comfortable talking about anything and quit going.

A few days later, Brynlee was at my apartment making herself a snack. She poured milk into her cereal and dropped the milk carton. Romeo lost it. He started screaming at her, screaming at me, threw the bowl of cereal across the room, and broke all of our kitchen chairs into various pieces. He went running out of the house, and I comforted Brynlee. I took her out to lunch, and we went and got our nails done. She told me she was scared of him but loved me so much. I just held her and cried, thinking to myself, *I feel the exact same way as you, little girl.* We came home later that afternoon. Romeo was grilling dinner; the chairs had been repaired to look like new, and he had bought Brynlee and I matching sparkly black UGG boots. All was right again—for Romeo. Another pattern that became the norm in our relationship.

The next morning we got up because we needed to take Brynlee back to her mom in Albert Lea. We dropped her off, and Romeo said that he wanted to stop by a friend's house and look at some tools he was selling. He told me to wait in the car. He came back out an hour later high as a kite. I asked what he used, and he said nothing. I asked again, and he said, "Heroin, baby."

I noticed we were not headed in the direction of home. I asked him where we were going, and he said to make some money. I did not ask any further questions. We went straight to a casino in southern Minnesota. I sat at a slot machine for about two hours while I waited for Romeo to do whatever it was he was doing. He eventually called my cell and asked me what I was doing and who I was talking to. His voice was loud, and his breathing was labored. I could tell just by the sound of his voice that he had mixed something with the heroin. I told him I was sitting playing slots, and he said, "I know. I am behind you, and I have been watching you for an hour."

I turned around and there he was, sweat pouring down his face, his body shaking. "We need to get the fuck out here before they get here," he said.

"Who?" I inquired.

"The Feds," Romeo said. "You better not be working with them."

I did not even know what to say. I just got up and walked out. It was really snowing, and the wind was picking up. I asked him if we could just get a room for the night. I did not want to leave with him driving in the condition that he was in, especially in a snowstorm. He just kept walking to our vehicle. I offered to drive, and he laughed. As we started off, the roads were terrible, even in our Jeep. I asked again if we could please just get a room.

"I will take off work tomorrow. It will be fun," I said.

Romeo slammed on the brakes. He got out, walked over to my door, grabbed my neck, and started pulling me out of the vehicle. I was fighting back and against the seat belt that was still attached to me. He eventually overpowered me, popped the seat belt release button, and dragged me out into the snowy darkness. He finally stopped and shoved me down alongside a steep hill on the side of the road. He got down on his knees and slammed my face hard onto the ground. I could see my blood seeping through the white snow.

"Look down there, bitch," he screamed. "If you ever turn on me or try to leave me, I will toss your dead body down this cliff, and no one will ever find you."

This was the first time he threatened to kill me and show me exactly where he would get rid of my body.

As soon as we got back to Minneapolis, Romeo dropped me off at home, indicating he had things he needed to do and asked if he could borrow some money. I told him no and went inside. I had decided after what happened that night that I was ending the relationship. I did not hear from him for two days. When he finally called, I told him I could not live like this, and it was over. He begged to come back home and that he would go to treatment. I called and talked to his mom. She convinced me to let him come back home and that she would help me find a treatment program and pay for it. I recognize now that his mom manipulated me a lot. But at the time, I had become so isolated that she was the only person I had to talk to about him. She loved her son, but was burned out from worrying about him night and day. She used me to take over the care of him.

Romeo came back home and sobered up once again. I scheduled an addiction screening for him, and we went together. He honestly participated in the screening, and I learned just how serious his addiction was. I learned more than I was ready to or capable of processing. He had been using illicit street drugs since he was 12 years old. He explained how he had crafted the ability to pass drug tests. I learned the arsenal of medications that he bought on the street to help him sleep and function. He used more drugs to help him deal with the negative effects of other drugs. I also learned that he had never actually completed a treatment program.

Afterward, Romeo completely broke down crying, explaining that he needed me, and the girls needed me, and he would do anything to get better. It was a three-week wait to get into a treatment center, and there was nothing anyone could do to make it happen any quicker. It was very hard to be around him over the next few days. He was going through severe withdrawals, was physically ill, and was very angry and unstable.

I came home from work one day to find him pacing through the house. I instantly thought he had used. He told me he needed money now. I responded that I was not giving him any money because I knew what he was going to do with it. He became volatile and said we were leaving for the casino. I went because, with Romeo, saying no was no longer an option, not that it ever really was. We got there and went up to a room. There were several people in the room. All eyes were on me. A guy came out of the bathroom and asked Romeo who the fuck I was as he handed him a bubble and they smoked meth together. He explained I was his girlfriend, and it was okay. No one seemed happy that I was there, and I was scared. Romeo and two other people went into the bathroom, and I watched them all hot rail heroin from a heated pipe. Hot railing heroin made Romeo crazy. I told him I wanted to leave. He could stay, but I wanted out of there. Before he could answer, there was a double knock at the door and another guy came in. When he saw Romeo, he suddenly ran up to him, grabbed him by the neck, and threw him up against the wall.

"You better have my money, you stupid fuck, or I am going to kill you right now," he said.

The other people in the room tried to calm him down. He then walked over to me and pulled out a gun.

"Who the fuck are you, bitch?"

Romeo immediately ran over and got between us. "She is my girlfriend and has nothing to do with this," he responded.

The guy shoved him out of the way and put the gun to my head and informed me that Romeo owed him thousands of dollars, and someone was going to get him the money tonight. I did not say a word.

Romeo went into the bathroom and came back out and told the guy he would be back in a few hours with the money, and we left. We got to the vehicle, and he pulled out a lot of those little plastic bags. This time I knew all too well what they were, and these were not empty. He started making calls and doing drops and "earning" the money he owed. Some places he stopped and went in, used, and then came back out. I thought about running when he left me in the vehicle, but I was on desolate tribal property and more scared of running than staying. He had also taken my phone as "insurance" that I would not do anything stupid.

After one of the last stops, I instantly knew Romeo had been hot railing again. He was wild and extremely paranoid. He came back to the vehicle and asked who had been inside. I said no one. He did not believe me.

"Someone has been in here. I smell cologne," he screamed.

Again, I told him no one had been in the fucking vehicle. He started driving fast, bobbing and weaving around parked cars until we hit a gravel road. We drove about a mile and then came up to a house with a large, fenced-in backyard.

He stopped the vehicle and grabbed me by the hair, smashed my forehead into the steering wheel, and said, "If you ever turn me in or tell anyone the things and people you now know, I will burn your body in that pit, bitch."

I believed him. That was the second time Romeo threatened to kill me and show me exactly where he would get rid of my body.

We spent the rest of the night finishing his sales, and then he went back to the casino to pay back a portion of what he owed. He dropped me off at home and then disappeared for a few days. I tried calling him several times. He had such a toxic hold on me by this time. I feared being with him as much as I feared leaving him. As hard as it may be to understand, knowing his whereabouts was safer for me than not knowing where he was or what he was doing because it was never good. Romeo knew a lot of dangerous people who knew who I was and where we lived. I knew a lot of information, and I believed that if he convinced himself that I was going to turn on him, he would follow through with his threats to kill me. I wanted to get him into treatment so that I could safely separate myself from him and clear my head from the insanity of what had become my everyday life. He never answered. Hours later, I would get a bizarre text, or he would call and then hang up when I answered. He missed a visit with Brynlee, so I went and picked her up. She asked where her dad was, and I just told her that he was out of town for work. I texted him many times that Brynlee was asking about him and that he needed to call us.

A few days later, he came home and went through another period of withdrawals and unstable behavior. We had a weekend planned at the lake with his family. He managed to somewhat pull himself together for that. Everyone knew he had relapsed, but life just went on as if he was fine. Only one more week before he could enter the in-patient treatment program. Romeo's relationship with his daughters had become very tense. Emma knew enough about her father's past to know that he was using drugs again. She passed on most scheduled visits. Brynlee was always worried about her daddy—why he was either gone or sleeping if he was around. I just kept lying to her. She and I became increasingly close, and I felt an overwhelming responsibility to protect her from all aspects of her relationship with Romeo.

The day before Romeo was to enter treatment, I was awakened in the middle of the night to someone pounding on our door. I heard Romeo yell, "Fuck!" from the living room. He burst into the bedroom and told me he needed cash now. I explained that I did not have any cash lying around, and it was 3:00 a.m., so what was I supposed to do? He told me to get into the closet and stay there. I heard him get on the phone to the person pounding on the door, explaining he would have his cash in a few hours but that his girl and daughter were in the house, so he told whoever he was talking to that he would meet him by noon with the money. He then came into the bedroom and told me we needed to get out of the house and go hustle whatever cash we could get together now. We went to the ATM, and I took out what I could, but it was not nearly close to what he owed. Romeo was raging and coming completely undone. He told me I better not be holding out on any cash, because now Mr. X knew where we lived in addition to knowing who I was, where I worked, and the vehicles we drove. I told him I did not have any more cash or any way to get money.

Romeo got busy. We drove from one side of Minneapolis to the other as he popped windows on vehicles and stole whatever he could. He then proceeded to go to every pawn shop he could find. I just sat there next to him, not knowing what to do or what to say. Being silent was the safest thing I could do. We met up with his dealer, and Romeo gave him all the cash that he was able to get together, and then we went home. Only one more day, and he would be in treatment, and I could get some time alone to collect my thoughts and figure out how I could safely end the relationship once and for all.

CHAPTER 3

HEROIN AND THE HEROINE

I woke up the following morning. Romeo, of course, had not come to bed. I knew today was going to be hard, as he had not wanted to talk much about treatment. I had been getting everything together that he would need. I got up and searched the house, but he was gone. I called his cell, and it went straight to voicemail. I frantically called his mom, who said she had not spoken to him in two days. I explained what had been happening the past few days. We were worried, especially knowing that he still had not paid back all the money he owed. I loved his mom. She was my only support and the only person I had that I could talk openly with about what life with Romeo was really like.

I called the treatment center, and they said they could not hold his bed because there was a waiting list, so I needed to get him there within 24 hours. Fucking great. I had no idea where he was, why his phone was off, if he was okay, or how I was going to get him to treatment in time. I did not hear from him for three days. He had turned his phone back on after the first day of going AWOL, and I could tell by our cell phone records that he had been making and receiving calls. I recognized some of the numbers and saw that he had called Brynlee's mom a couple of times, so he was at least alive. That was our weekend to have Brynlee. I tried to reach her mother but could not. I finally received a phone call from Romeo early on Sunday morning. He was having difficulty breathing and was screaming manically, but I could not understand what he was saying. I kept trying to calm him down so that I could understand him. He kept hanging up and then calling back. I called his mom and asked her to try and get a hold of him, but he would not answer her calls.

Finally, after an hour, I figured out that he needed me to come get him and Brynlee from a well-known trap house/drug hotel. (A trap house is a house or sometimes a hotel where addicts regularly gather to buy, sell, and use.) I knew where it was because it was not the first or second or 10th time that I had to pick him up from there. I waited in the vehicle for 30 minutes, but they did not come out, so I knew I was going to have to go in and get them. You see, you do not under any circumstance contact the police when you are trying to get a loved one out of a trap house. Trap houses are extremely dangerous. Most people have guns, and it can get ugly fast. If it had just been Romeo, I would have left like I had done countless times before if I couldn't convince him on the phone to come out. But knowing Brynlee was inside, I had no choice but to go in. I let his mom know the address and that she should start driving to Minneapolis in case I did not call her back in 30 minutes. I went into the hotel and to the room number that he usually stayed in there. I heard several people's voices inside. I yelled through the door that I was Romeo's girl, and I was here to pick him and his daughter up. I heard a woman yelling Romeo's name, and then I heard Brynlee's voice; she was crying. I yelled through the door to her that it was me and to come out. I heard someone else yelling at Romeo that I better not be a fucking cop.

I finally heard him scream, "She's my girl."

He then opened the door, and I scooped up Brynlee in my arms and ran back to the vehicle. It was freezing cold, and she had no shoes or coat. Romeo was a mess. I had never seen him this bad.

I did not know what to do, but he ran out with us and jumped into the vehicle, screaming, "We need to get the fuck out of here now!"

I called his mom and told her I had them both, so she did not need to come. I went to the nearest gas station and got Brynlee something to eat and drink. I did not feel safe going home because I didn't know if someone was really after him, and I did not want anyone else knowing where we lived, so I checked the three of us into a hotel so that I could figure out what to do next. Romeo had track marks all over his body. He was shaking and moaning. It literally made me sick to my stomach to see him like this. I took Brynlee into the bathroom and gave her a bath. I asked her some questions to make sure she was okay and that no one had hurt her. She said she had fun with Daddy, but then they had to go to that scary hotel, and no one would let Daddy leave. She said she just wanted me, so Daddy said he would call me to come help them. I told her that we would go shopping for some warm clothes as soon as the stores opened, and she could pick where she wanted to eat. I then got her tucked in bed to watch TV.

I tried talking to Romeo. He was curled up on the other bed continuing to just moan and twitch uncontrollably. It took me most of the day to track down Brynlee's mom. I told her what happened. She said she knew Romeo was using but did not think he was as bad off as he was and figured I would be around, so she let him take Brynlee. She came to Minneapolis and picked her up that evening. I went back to the hotel, and Romeo was in worse shape than when I had left him. I started Googling withdrawals and trying to educate myself on what to do. I got him into the bathtub and did my best, but eventually had to call 911 to come help me because I thought he was going to die in front of me. I tried to get him committed on a 72-hour hold in the hospital but was unable to. He came back home with me and slept for a couple of days. When he finally came to some sort of normal level of functioning, I told him I could not be a part of this lifestyle anymore and that he never should have picked up Brynlee that weekend, let alone bring her to a trap house. He began to cry and begged me not to leave him.

"I don't want to be like this. Why am I like this? I just want to be normal. Please, please help me. I don't want to die like this. I hate myself more than you could ever hate me right now," he repeated over and over.

It is unbearable watching someone you deeply love be trapped in the throes of drug addiction. They are fighting for their life in front of you. And there is nothing you can do but stand by and watch their disease take everything from them. Addiction is a cunning disease, and the severity of Romeo's addiction was like nothing I had seen or read about after 15 years of sitting in courtrooms, reading hundreds of chemical assessments, and knowing clients who had lost their lives to addiction. The range of emotions I had exhausts me to even think about now. I do not know how I was even functioning at that point. Keeping up with the demands of my job, taking care of Romeo, trying to protect the girls and keep them and myself safe was too much. I was breaking under the pressure, but I loved him so much and was beginning to have insight into what it was like living in his head every day. Living with addiction and untreated mental health is debilitating. I didn't see Romeo as a frightening addict. I saw him as a frightening man with a dangerous addiction problem. A clean Romeo and a drug-using Romeo were two entirely different people. The good doesn't disappear. The belief that if given proper treatment, the good can resurface doesn't disappear. It does grow dimmer. The dichotomy of fearing and loving the same person steals your soul and leaves you falling further and further down that dark hole an addict has spent their whole life trying to get out of. Seeing him with this very sincere remorse, pain, fear, and passionate desire to be someone he could not be all just further added to the toxicity and complexity of our relationship.

I called the treatment center and explained that I could bring him right then, but they said all the beds were taken, so I would need to find somewhere else or get back on the waiting list. I called his mom and asked her to start calling around again. She said she would and that she would also have his sister help. We were unable to get him in anywhere before he disappeared again. It was a week before I heard from him next. He called indicating that he taken too much this time and would be dying soon. I do not know if he had or not, but I believed he thought he was dying. He was pleading with me to make sure the girls knew how much he loved them and how sorry he was for being so fucked up. The phone went dead. I contacted the police to see if there was any way that they could get a location from his cell phone or help me locate him. They said there was nothing they could do. Romeo called about six hours later asking for money, having no memory of the previous phone call we had.

Over the next month, it was basically the same. He would call telling me he was being chased by police or had a hit man after him or that he was going to shoot himself or that he was dying from dirty drugs. The scary part was all those scenarios could easily be true at any given time. I changed the locks on the door and kept a watchful eye on my surroundings at all times. I was scared of Romeo, but I was also scared of the people that he owed money to. I lost track of how many times I was followed when I left the house or when I had to stop by the office. While I worked from home, there were still times I needed to go in for a meeting or to have work done on my laptop. I know Romeo also had people following me to keep tabs on what I was doing because he told me so. I was constantly receiving phone calls from people looking for him or telling me he needed me to come get him. I tried several times to meet up with him, but he never was where he told me he would be. He called one night to say he would be home in the morning with Brynlee. I immediately called Brynlee's mother to inform her that under no circumstance should she let her be alone with him. Her mother had her own issues with drug addiction, so I had little trust that she would do what was best. She looked for any chance she could to get Brynlee out of the house. The next day Romeo did attempt to come home while I was gone and was furious that the locks had been changed. He gave me 15 minutes to get home, or he was going to take Brynlee and leave town for good. I immediately went home. He was disheveled, dirty, shaking uncontrollably, and Brynlee was crying hysterically. He immediately started going through the house looking for the undercover police that he was convinced I had there waiting for him. I told him he needed to leave Brynlee with me and get out of the house. He refused to leave, as he now convinced himself that I had police/DEA outside waiting for him. I told him that we needed to call his mom so that she could come and pick up Brynlee. He eventually agreed that we could meet his mom in St. Cloud, Minnesota, to drop her off.

This was a painfully heartbreaking drive. I did not even know who Romeo was anymore. He was unrecognizable to the man I fell in love with a year ago. By this time, he had lost over 70 pounds, had open sores all over his face, and was covered from neck to toes in track marks. I have also never seen him so strung out before. It was 10 below out, and he was wearing nothing but a stained white tank top full of holes, jeans that were not his own, because a clean Romeo would never have worn that brand, and tennis shoes that were too big for his feet. His hands, nails, and face were filthy dirty. He smelled awful. His whole body was shaking uncontrollably. Brynlee was crying in the backseat asking her dad over and over again what was wrong with him and then started asking me what was wrong with him and if Daddy was dying.

Romeo was convinced that we were being followed and that I was up to something. He made me pull over on the freeway every time headlights popped up behind us so that he could be assured that the vehicle was not following us. I wanted to be mad at him. I wanted to hate him. But I could not. He truly believed every crazy thought he was having was actually happening in real life. He was hearing things—voices. He kept screaming at Brynlee to shut off her toys; she didn't have any toys or even a stuffed animal. He was sweating and his heart was racing. He kept opening the window to get fresh air in. He kept locking and unlocking the doors over and over and over. Then he started saying he should just jump out and kill himself. I was very worried that he would do that. Romeo told me many times he wanted to die because he could not keep living like he was, but he also had an immense fear of dying alone. He had told me countless times that we would die together because he would need me to be with him. We finally made it to the exit. I took it and picked up my phone to call his mom to see how close she was. He grabbed my phone and asked me why I had a new phone. I tried explaining it was not new; it was the same phone I had for the past year. He screamed that I was a liar and threw my phone out the window. Trying not to escalate him any further with Brynlee in the vehicle, I told him to call his mom. He went silent, completely checked out from reality. Then suddenly he started mumbling that he had it all figured out.

"Stop the fucking vehicle, now, bitch," he screamed.

I pleaded with him to just get Brynlee to his mom.

"I know you are lying. My mom isn't even coming, is she? You have been setting me up this whole time. How long have you been working for the Feds?" he screamed.

I kept telling him I had no idea what he was talking about. He told me to get out of the vehicle. I got out and went to the back seat to pick up Brynlee, who was crying uncontrollably by this time. He ran around and shoved me to the ground. I told him I was just trying to comfort Brynlee. He took her out of her car seat, and she immediately ran over to me, and I picked her up and told her everything was okay, that I loved her, and we were all going to be fine. I started praying that another car would drive by soon so that I could get some help. I looked up to see what Romeo was doing. He had opened all the doors and the back of my Jeep. He was tearing the vehicle apart, pulling out wires and cords. He then completely punched out my already shattered radio and dissected every tiny piece of it. He proceeded to get down on the ground, using the flashlight on his phone, and started sifting through everything that he had pulled out and destroyed. I just stood there not knowing what to do or say.

Finally, I said, "Please call your mom. We are freezing."

He said to get into the vehicle. I put Brynlee back in her car seat and got into the driver's side. He told me he was driving, so I got into the passenger seat. He looked at me and broke down and started crying, saying he was sorry and then asked where we were and why we were there. I told him he was on a very bad trip and that I was scared, and Brynlee was scared.

"We need to call your mom to help us. You threw my phone out the window."

He handed me his phone, and I called his mom and told her that I needed to figure out where we were, but that we would meet her at a hotel parking lot in a few minutes. When we got there, Romeo told me to take Brynlee over to his mom because he did not want her to see him like this. I asked his mom to please take Romeo with her. I was done. "I cannot take it anymore," I told her. She said that she could not do that and to just get him and myself back home, and then she drove off with Brynlee, leaving me alone with him. I went back to my vehicle and told Romeo that he should not be driving and to please just let me drive home. He agreed.

All the way back to Minneapolis, he sat humming and twitching in the seat next to me, a million miles away, clicking the door lock over and over and over. And having loud conversations with imaginary people that he honestly thought were sitting next to him. At one point, he started throwing punches into the air as if he were actually in a physical fight with someone.

I was scared to go home with him, so I said, "I assume there is somewhere you need me to drop you off?"

"The casino." He said, "I need to take care of some things."

So I dropped him off and went home not knowing when or if I would ever see him again. Or wanted to.

About a week later, he called and said that he needed money, but not for drugs, because he had not paid that restitution and only had a day left to get it paid. I assumed he was lying, and then I did what I should have done a long time ago. I ran a complete criminal background check on him. Romeo had been truthful that he had been in trouble when he was in his 20s, but he neglected to tell me about all the serious criminal trouble he had consistently been in ever since. He did indeed have a felony theft case, and a warrant had already been issued for unpaid restitution. I called him back and said I would think about getting the money together so that I could buy myself some time to think about what my next move would be. I called his mom and we decided that if we could locate him, we would contact law enforcement and have him arrested so that we could get him into a long-term in-patient treatment program through the county. Romeo called back later telling me he did not know where he was, but that I needed to come help him. I tried to piece together all the usual places to check, but I could not find him anywhere. I would have to wait until he was off this trip to try and narrow it down. He called the next day, and I told him that I had spoken with his mom, and we would get the money together to help him pay off his restitution. He asked if a warrant had been issued yet, and I lied and said no. He told me he had some things to take care of and that he would call me later to set up a time and place to meet. This game went on for weeks. I would constantly be checking phone records to see if his phone had been active, but it was over five days with no activity. I was fearing the worst. But, he called later that night from a different phone number telling me that law enforcement in another county was now looking for him because of some new thefts and a forged check. I told him that he needed to turn himself in, or this was going to spiral out of control, and he would end up never seeing his daughters again. He asked if he could come hide out at home for a few days until we could figure out a plan. I told him that he could, but that I needed to pick him up as I did not want anyone to follow him to our home. As soon as he told me where he was, I could contact the police to arrest him. We went back and forth like this for a couple more weeks.

One night, I received a phone call from yet another police department asking me if I knew Romeo. I said yes, and they told me he had just been arrested along with a woman who had my driver's license and a credit card of mine in her purse. I felt so many things during this phone call. I was relieved Romeo was not dead, confused as to why he had been arrested, and without any idea whatsoever who this woman was or how in the hell she had my personal belongings. The officer told me that he would call me in the morning and sort things out. He also informed me that Romeo had two other warrants out for his arrest in Minnesota and two more in North Dakota, so he would be safely kept in county jail for quite some time.

After sobering up in jail for a week, Romeo started calling. I watched the calls for days, not answering, but he was relentless. I eventually picked up, and we talked. I knew better than to ever have picked up that fucking phone, but I did it anyway over and over. Slowly but surely, he was conning his way back into my life—the sound of his voice, the remorse, the sadness, the reliving of the good times, the demons he was fighting, the pressure from his mom to stay in contact with him for the sake of the girls, and the overwhelming love I had in the depths of my soul for this man and those little girls. Romeo bounced from county jail to county jail dealing with all his active warrants. He was struggling with very serious withdrawals and depression and was put on suicide watch a couple of times. I went to see him several times in the various jails and helped him arrange phone calls with the girls.

Eventually, he was sentenced to 14 months in prison. His mom and I went to his final sentencing hearing together and watched as he was led away in shackles to spend his last couple of nights in county jail before being shipped off to prison. I remember sitting in that courtroom afterward trying to comprehend how in the fuck I ended up there. All those years, I was the attorney, owning the courtroom. And now I was sitting in the "audience," crying as the man I loved was in an orange jumpsuit on his way to prison. The past two years of my life did not seem real, yet it all was. And no matter what that man put me through, I was still madly in love with him. His mom and I walked out together in silence.

She gave me a hug, and she asked, "What now?"

And I responded, "I am finally going to get on with my life and somehow find a way to get over Romeo. It should be easy now that he is going to be in prison."

CHAPTER 4

RIDE OR DIE

Romeo called every day he was in jail waiting to find out what prison he would be transferred to. He was concerned about me, his mom, and the girls. Emma knew her dad was going to prison and sadly wasn't overly upset about it. She had seen and experienced a lot with him over the years and had already emotionally distanced herself from him. Brynlee was more difficult. We were unsure what her mom was going to tell her, and so Romeo's mom and I decided that we would wait until one of us talked to her and then go from there. His mom was actually relieved he was going to prison because she no longer had to worry about him. I did not know how to process all that happened over the course of our relationship, let alone this. I shared his mom's sense of relief in many ways. I was exhausted. I wanted to get back into a normal, healthy routine—back to that "boring" life from what seemed like a lifetime ago, before I fell in love with Romeo.

He called the next day and said that he was being sent to prison in Moose Lake, Minnesota, which was two hours from where we were living, and asked me to come see him once before he was shipped off. I agreed to do so. I had mentally prepared myself for the conversation that I intended to have with him, specifically, what I was going to tell him—that I wished him well and that I really hoped for his sake and the girls that he utilized whatever treatment and mental health programs were available so that he could come home and rebuild relationships with those little girls I so deeply loved. For me, I was going to move on, and in order to do so, I needed no contact with him. I rehearsed the speech like I was preparing for one of my opening arguments in a trial. Romeo had been moved to an actual prison in St. Cloud, Minnesota, where all inmates are temporarily held until they reach their permanent prison "homes." That was the first time I had ever been inside of a prison. Prisons are very different from all the county jails I had been in and out of the last few months with Romeo and over the course of my career in criminal law. It was eerie, dark, and exceedingly depressing. I had assumed that I would be talking to him from a divided room on a phone or through an intercom system, but in prison, unless you are a high-risk inmate, the visits are in person. This really threw me off. I walked into the visitation area and saw Romeo from across the room. The guard had told me that I could hug him when I first got there and when I left, but the rest of the time I needed to remain seated in the chair across from him. That was the first time in four months that I was going to touch him or feel his arms around me. I was not prepared for the emotions, neither his nor mine. As soon as I got close enough, Romeo hugged me tight, and we both broke down into tears and just sat crying and looking at each other. I wanted to scream at him. I wanted to tell him how much I hated him for everything he put me through, but the only words that came unconsciously out of my mouth were, "I love you so much, and this hurts so deeply."

Romeo began to try and explain what happened from the beginning of that very first relapse and how he was able to hide it from me for so long because he could control his use until it reached a point where he no longer had the ability to do so. He tried stopping so many times but could not. He also did not remember a lot of what happened or just remembered fragments. The look on his face, the pain and shame when I started filling him in on all his missing pieces. I cannot even begin to imagine what it is like in the head of an addict when they get clean for the first time after a relapse like Romeo had and to have to listen to and process the things they did and the pain and trauma they caused the people they love. He became physically sick and told me that he could not hear anymore. He then began to apologize and tell me how much he loved me and reminded me that I was the only person in his entire life that believed there was some good inside of him and that he needed me to keep believing that. I watched a man that I loved more than anyone I had ever loved turn into an unrecognizable, terrifying monster— someone that I was extremely afraid of, but yet still believed that separate from the addiction, underneath it all, was a man who was wildly exciting, gentle, protective, and loving. I no longer looked at him the same way I did when I first met him, but I was still enthralled and addicted to him. He had a hold on me that at the time I did not understand. It was powerful and all-consuming.

We suddenly heard the announcement that there were two minutes left of visitation. Romeo stood up, held me tight, and told me how much he loved me and for me to please wait for him and give him a chance to show me who he really was capable of being.

"We will get married, and I will provide you and the girls with the life you deserve," he said.

The guard then led him away. He looked back and yelled across the room, "I love you more than life, babe. Do not ever forget that."

I walked out of that prison to my vehicle and sat in the parking lot crying for two hours. I called his mom and she asked me what I was going to do, and I told her I did not know. She reminded me how much he loved me and how much the girls loved me and that she would always be there for me no matter what.

"Romeo is alive and not another overdose statistic because you loved him and protected him and gave him a reason to stay alive all those nights he was on death's door. I have never seen my son look at anyone the way he looks at you. You two have a powerful connection, and I am not sure either one of you is going to ever be able to let that go," she said.

Fuck, I thought, *I am not so sure either*.

Three days later, Romeo called from his new home, Moose Lake Prison. He was handling it much better than I could have ever anticipated. He was calm and shared with me what it was like getting settled in. I actually believe that there was a part of him that took comfort in the security of his surroundings, and that is a hard concept for someone to wrap their head around. He told me that he had already mailed me the paperwork I needed to complete to be put on the approved visitation list. Meanwhile, I was settling into a peaceful routine at home and started back up with attending various support group meetings for family members of addicts to help me process everything that had gone on.

Romeo and I spoke every day and usually a couple of times a day. His mom called to see how he was doing. I asked why she had not spoken to him. She told me she had been through this once before, and he had me so I could keep her informed on how he was doing. I explained that I was talking to him now, but I was not sure if I was going to be able to continue to do so because it was emotionally draining. I asked her if she had received the paperwork for visitation.

She said, "I will let you have all the visitation time."

I explained that I had not even decided if I was going to visit him, but she told me I needed to. He needed someone, and the girls would feel better knowing I was seeing their daddy.

"You should call Emma's mom and get permission from her to be able to bring her down to see her dad, and you need to call Brynlee's mom because Brynlee is wondering where her daddy is and how many more days until she gets to come see you."

I hung up the phone and started to cry. I was so torn on what to do. I loved Romeo, those little girls, and his mom so much. I mailed in the visitation paperwork, and within a week, he had let me know that I had been approved for visitation and that I could come that weekend. He started crying and begging that I just come see him at least once. He had something he wanted to tell me and could not wait to hug me. I missed him deeply, at least the man I fell in love with, and I missed his arms around me. I was an addict who needed a hit.

The following Saturday I got up early and headed down to Moose Lake. It was a four-hour round trip, and visitation would be 60 minutes. I drove through the prison gates and up to the visitation building. The parking lot was empty except for one other car. I was beginning to think Romeo had told me the wrong time, as I anticipated that there would be a lot of people there visiting their loved ones. I walked in, got patted down and searched. I then went through the metal detector and was told that I was not going to be able to see Romeo because I had an underwire bra on. I thought it was a joke. The guards had zero patience for my naivety, and I was frustrated. The only other woman in the entire room walked up to me and said she had a sports bra in her car and that I could have it so that I could still see Romeo. She got it for me, I changed, and, finally, got cleared to go in.

I walked into the visitation room, and Romeo popped up from the chair he was sitting in. Only

Romeo could look like a million dollars wearing a white T-shirt and elastic-waisted jeans in a goddamn prison visitation room. My heart did flip flops, and my stomach was in knots. I walked over to him, and he grabbed me tight. We sat and talked for the hour. He explained that his case manager had told him that he would be starting treatment in two weeks, and he had also voluntarily agreed to start a long-term anger management program. I told him I was glad he was taking some responsibility finally and would be using his time wisely. We laughed. We reminisced. We cried. When it was time to leave, he held me tight and told me how much he loved me and appreciated that I came to see him. He told me he would call me later, as I had arranged for him to talk to both girls, as they were with his mom that weekend at the lake. It was very surreal walking away from him. Of course, I wished he could come home with me. He was clean; he was back to his charming, witty self. He had put on at least half the 70 pounds he had lost during the last relapse and had the sparkle back in those addicting brown eyes. I got back to my vehicle and drove home in silence, still wearing some strange woman's non-underwire bra thinking what in the actual fuck am I doing still wildly in love with this man.

Over the course of the next 10 months, I spoke to Romeo almost every day and went to see him every single weekend. We wrote letters back and forth and were planning life for when he came home. Yes, Romeo and I were going to resume life together and start over. He told me he had completed a nine-month drug treatment program and was going to

NA meetings every day. (I later found out that was a lie.) He also told me that he had completed his anger management program and told me in great detail what he had learned and that he had been put on two different medications to deal with his mental health issues. (Also lies.) We had open discussions about several of the most traumatic things that happened between us, including the physical abuse. He apologized over and over again, convincing me that it was the addiction causing the behavior and that I needed to work on forgiving him so that we could have a clean slate when he came back home.

Finally, the day had arrived when Romeo was being released. I had driven to Moose Lake the night before, as I could get the call any time after 6:00 a.m. that it was time to pick him up. I was pacing around the hotel, butterflies in my stomach and heart racing. He finally called and I went over to the prison. He looked like the old Romeo but was now in better physical and mental health than he had ever been, or so I thought. I got out of my vehicle. He dropped his box of belongings and ran across the parking lot to me, swooped me up in his arms, and kissed me. It was like kissing him for the first time all over again. I had moved during the time he had been away, so he was excited to see our new place. We knew none of his clothes would fit, as he had not only gained all his weight back, but he had been lifting and running so he was looking forward to getting some new clothes, getting back to work, and being able to build our new life together. His mom had been promising to help me financially with things when he came home, but never followed through with so much as a dollar or a single piece of clothing. Fortunately for Romeo, I had been working a tremendous amount of overtime while he was gone so I could afford to get him what he needed for a fresh start.

I had taken a three-week vacation from work so that we had time together and with the girls to help make his transition back into home life go as smoothly as possible. I also knew that we would need to share a vehicle until he got on his feet, as his truck had been seized by the police during his last arrest. I learned another very hard lesson with Romeo, that transition from prison life to real life is extremely complicated for both the parolee and their loved ones. He did not know how to function without the rigid, controlled environment of prison life. The honeymoon phase lasted about 48 hours. Romeo immediately wanted to drink. I was surprised considering he had been in an intense treatment program. I tried talking to him about it, and he said that he would never touch drugs again, but that a few beers were always going to be part of his life and that he knew how to "work the system" when it came to UA testing and for me to quit worrying about everything. I could tell he was really having a lot of anxiety. I asked where the medication was that he had been taking for the past year. He told me that the prison would not let him leave with it, so he would need to find a doctor as soon as he had health insurance. I called him mom and said that she needed to send him some money immediately because I could not continue to cover the cost of everything, and he needed his medications now, not three months from now. She agreed and sent money.

Romeo told me that he would call that day and get in somewhere. I believed him and did not give it much thought afterward. I was busy organizing a surprise family get-together at the lake the following day. We had not told the girls that Romeo was out yet and wanted to surprise them in person. He was busy making phone calls about jobs and trying to settle into some sort of routine.

The next day we went to the lake. Other than Brynlee, no one seemed to care he was home, nor did Romeo seem particularly interested in seeing anyone either. I was struck by how odd and sad this was for everyone. He knew rebuilding his family relationships was going to take time and effort, especially with Emma, and I sensed immediately that this was not going to be a priority for him. We had to leave that same night, as he had a job interview the next morning. I had talked to his mom and stepdad about them giving him a loan so that he could get a used truck, and they both said not a chance and that he and I would have to figure that out on our own. Romeo got the first job he applied for and was starting work the next day. We tried sharing a vehicle, but it simply was not possible with our different work schedules and living in a big city. I used money I had built up in savings and bought him a used truck. He lasted at his first job about three weeks and then quit. He was depressed and drinking a lot. He found a new job and quit that one after a few days, indicating that some of the other guys were using drugs, and he could not be around that. This pattern continued for the next two months, but Romeo eventually found a job that he liked and was a good fit for him. He came home one day and told me that we needed to buy this old Harley he had found because he wanted to take me to Sturgis the following month. I agreed that it was a great idea. We had been talking about going to Sturgis since the day we met. I also thought it would be something fun for us to do together and a way for him and I to start making some mutual friends. I bought the used bike the following week, and we started making plans with another couple for our first Sturgis motorcycle rally.

Romeo seemed to be settling into a calmer existence and was busy planning our trip. It gave him something to focus on. He worked a lot of overtime so that he had money to fix up the bike the way he wanted to and buy us all the things we needed for the trip. We connected on an even higher level when we were riding. Riding cleared the demons from his head. As most bikers do, Romeo connected to the bike and to me. When he hit the open road, he relaxed and enjoyed the peace as the voices in his head were lulled into silence by the roar of the bike. We would ride and just get lost in life together.

We made memories of a lifetime on that trip to Sturgis. While Romeo vice gripped his addiction every moment of every day, that had been the longest period of being clean that he had experienced in his entire adult life. For the first time, I felt a sense of peace and safety with him. I believed that the worst was behind us, and my dream of our family life was coming to fruition. It still deeply worried me that he was not working any sort of recovery program, but I convinced myself that the treatment he had gone through in prison had worked to the extent possible.

By the following spring, Brynlee's mom was basically out of the picture due to her drug addiction and criminal issues, so it was decided that Brynlee would come live with us for the summer. Romeo was not used to being a full-time parent. He was constantly making excuses as to why he could neither take her to nor pick her up from the summer daycare camp I had enrolled her in. He was back to becoming very short-fused with me and with her. Brynlee was happy to be living with me and would often tell me I was her mommy and she never wanted to leave. I loved this little girl so much. She filled my mothering void, and I gave her the protection and love that she desperately needed. I never once said a bad word about her mother to her. I was very careful to make sure that she understood that she was a little girl who had two mommies that loved her.

Romeo started coming home later and later, always saying that he and the guys were having a few beers after work like all men, and if I did not like it, too bad. One night he came home extremely intoxicated and tripped over Brynlee's backpack that was sitting by the door. He went ballistic in the house, throwing and breaking everything in sight. Brynlee started crying in her room, so I got up to go in and comfort her. He grabbed me by the neck and smashed my head into the wall and told me that I needed to start giving him some space or this "relationship" was not going to work. I recognized the behavior, his body movements, his choice of words, and knew he was under the influence of more than alcohol. I spent the rest of the night sleeping in bed with Brynlee. The following morning, he was sitting on the couch buried in his phone. Brynlee and I quietly got ready for our day and left. I did not hear from him all day, and he was not home when Brynlee and I got home that evening. I called his mom and told her what happened. She tried to get a hold of him but could not.

He called about 11:00 p.m. that night and said he needed me to come pick him up right away. I could not leave Brynlee alone, so I got her up and we went to pick him up at some automotive garage. He was a mess. He told me that he had fucked up and used cocaine with co-workers. I brought him home and told Brynlee that Daddy had the flu. I called his mom back, and she said that maybe it was time that Romeo and I move out of Minneapolis. She had convinced herself, and eventually us, that getting out of the large city and into a tiny, rural community would help him stay clean. There were too many temptations and using friends for him in Minneapolis. Isolating him and limiting his opportunities to buy and use drugs would therefore make life easier for him.

Over the next several weeks, Romeo repeated this same pattern over and over again. One night, I received a phone call from someone that I needed to come pick him up from that same automotive garage because he thought Romeo had overdosed, and no one there would be calling for help. After he had slept that off for three days, we sat down and talked. I told him that under no circumstances was I going to allow Brynlee to be around this, nor was I ever going to go down this road again with him. He started crying and said he had some things he needed to tell me. He never attended anger management classes or treatment of any kind in prison, nor had he ever been prescribed any medications. It had all been lies. He said he had been using cocaine for many weeks and combining it with downers and drinking to hide it, but that he shot (needles) cocaine that night he threw me against the wall and had done so again the other night, but the dope was dirty, and he had a bad reaction. He said he was very scared and did not want this to be happening.

We packed up for the weekend and went to the lake to have a family meeting with his mom. Everyone except me thought that the solution to Romeo's addiction was for me to give up my entire life in Minneapolis so that he could have a fighting chance at staying clean in a small community. I am sure that down deep I knew that was never going to be possible, but I felt that in order to keep my family intact, it is what I needed to do. I didn't want to lose Romeo, and more importantly, I did not want to lose Brynlee. In many ways, I shared his mom's thought process that if we could make it harder for him to use, we could keep him clean. I also thought that having his family close to us would inspire him to want to make them proud by making good decisions and settling down into traditional family life— something he had yearned for his whole life.

He secured a good job with a high-end construction company and found us a house to rent in a very tiny town outside of Nisswa, Minnesota. I was able to convince my employer to allow me to work remotely, and within a month, we had moved. It was a very difficult transition for me. I deeply missed Minneapolis. I also hated working from home in such a remote area. I felt painfully isolated from the world. Romeo was loving it. We quickly made beautiful friendships with the people in our small community. We lived about 10 minutes from his mom and stepfather, which was very good for all of us. Romeo established a relationship with his stepfather for the first time in his life.

Brynlee's mother was spiraling fast, and Child Protective Services became involved. They wanted to know if Romeo and I wanted to pursue getting custody of her. Romeo proposed to me shortly thereafter on a weekend snowmobile trip and told me that he was also ready to step up as a father and pursue getting permanent custody of Brynlee. While on the surface, things were better between us than they had been since his last relapse, underneath, he was really struggling. Vice gripping addiction (which means refraining from use with no support and just using sheer will power) was wearing on him in very unsettling ways. He was often moody and depressed and then would turn very manic and recklessly impulsive. He was spending way beyond our means, and nothing ever seemed to satisfy him for very long. While he liked the sound of having Brynlee living with us, he was not interested in being a full-time father any more than he was when we lived in Minneapolis. He was drinking heavily and was exhibiting every sign of verging on another relapse. He refused to seek any help, and his demons were fighting hard, and he was becoming emotionally unstable. There was a very apparent decline in his mental health, and I was starting to feel unsettled being around him in a way I had never felt before.

People started asking me what was wrong with him and if I was safe. He had been verbally abusive to me in front of many of our friends.

One night, he came home from work and asked me if I was seeing someone else. I told him of course not and where would he possibly get an idea like that. He said he wanted to go out for a few beers. Romeo was never content with just sitting home. We constantly had to be doing something all of the time. This had only gotten worse after moving to a small town. I told him I had already made dinner and did not really feel like going out. He dragged me into the bedroom by my neck and told me to get ready, so I did. He was extremely agitated all night and socially distanced from everyone in the little bar we were in. A mutual male friend came up to pull me aside and ask if everything was okay. I lied like always and replied that everything was fine.

Romeo immediately came over, grabbed the beer out of my hand, slammed it on the table, and said, "We are fucking leaving right now, you cheating bitch."

I looked at the bartender, who was a good friend of ours, and she told me to stay and not leave with him. I wanted to stay, but I left with him.

We got home and Romeo threw the dinner I had made across the room, flipped over the couch, and started smashing the kitchen chairs while mumbling why does everyone think he is still a junkie. I asked him what he was talking about, and he just started to scream. I ran away and locked myself in the upstairs bathroom. I knew he had started seeing those red visions again.

The following weekend was Father's Day. Romeo, Brynlee, and I planned to go down to Minneapolis, pick up Emma, and then spend the weekend at a waterpark hotel. The girls were so excited. Romeo got up early and said he was going to take the Harley and run a quick errand in town while Brynlee and I got ready. Emma had called twice to see if we had left yet. After an hour, I called him, but his phone was shut off. I instantly got a very sick feeling in my stomach. Hours went by and nothing. His mom was calling him, Emma was calling him, and his sister was calling him. Brynlee was getting very worried about where her dad was. I lied and told her that he had probably stopped by a job site and lost track of time. She said she wanted to go look for him, so we did. I drove everywhere, but there was no sign of him. Emma was angry and so hurt, Brynlee was crying, and the rest of us were both pissed and worried. He had to have been in an accident, right? Not even Romeo would intentionally abandon his daughters on Father's Day, right? His mom decided to drive down to Minneapolis, pick up Emma, and bring her to the lake cabin until we could find Romeo. I told her I would take Brynlee into town for dinner, and then we could all meet up together later in the evening.

As Brynlee and I were on our way back home, I received a phone call from a friend who told me there was a man that looked like Romeo running in the ditch about a mile from where I was and that my Harley was parked on the highway. As I approached the intersection, I saw squad cars everywhere. I saw my Harley and then I saw Romeo being held down by two officers. I immediately yelled at Brynlee to lie down in the back seat and not get up until I said so. She started crying. I explained to her that there was a hurt animal on the road, and I did not want her to see it. Un-fucking-believable. I was watching the tow truck hook up my bike and my fiancé be shoved into the back of a squad car while his daughter was hysterically crying in the backseat.

I got home and calmed Brynlee down and had her start watching her favorite movie. I called Romeo's mom and told her what I knew. As I was talking to her, I got another call. It was the local police department. They informed me that Romeo had been arrested for felony DWI and reckless driving. They told me my Harley was going to be impounded because it was a felony DWI. If Brynlee was not in my care, I would have literally packed up my belongings and left that night. Romeo called for two days straight, and I refused to answer. His mom and I decided that we needed to tell Emma the truth, and for Brynlee, we made up some extravagant lie like always. Romeo had court on Monday morning and was released on conditional bail. His court-ordered condition of release was a breathalyzer. This breathalyzer was a portable device that Romeo had to carry with him at all times. He would receive a phone call at various times of the day and night where he would be required to blow into the device to prove that he had no alcohol in his body. As long as he remained sober, he could remain free until his next court hearing. If he did not remain sober, a warrant would be immediately issued for his arrest. His mom went to town to pick him up, but his stepfather would not allow him to stay with them, so she dropped him off at home. Romeo came in and proceeded to tell me that he was overwhelmed with work, Brynlee's custody case, and his never-ending desire to get high. He went on to say that he had just needed to let off some steam, so he decided to go riding and drinking with friends. He said he only planned to be gone for a few hours and then was going to come home so that we could leave.

For the first time, I just looked at him, really looked at him, and thought to myself what a piece of shit he truly was. How could anyone do that to their daughters, especially considering how strained his relationship was with both of them? He told me that he knew he could not drink anymore and had completed the chemical assessment that the county had offered him and would agree to go to any treatment facility that we could find. We were already financially over-extended; he had just lost the only asset we could liquidate—my Harley—and we were only a few months away from Brynlee's final custody hearing, as her mom had now been sentenced to a year in jail.

I was at a breaking point. I did not know what to think, let alone do. I was trapped and I just wanted to run away. I know that Romeo was remorseful, but his remorse was not enough this time. I talked to his mom, and she convinced me to keep riding it out because of Brynlee and because Romeo needed me more now than ever because no one wanted to see Brynlee end up in foster care.

Romeo was struggling hard to stay sober from alcohol, and his mental health was deteriorating even more quickly. Staying clean from drugs was already painfully difficult for him, let alone now also not being able to drink. He was working long days to keep busy and help get some cash together so that he could buy a used Harley to replace mine, which he did a few weeks later. I was troubled by how fast he came up with that much cash. I asked a few times, to which he responded, "Just been working hard, babe." I knew that was not the truth but just turned a blind eye because I did not want to know. His attorney for the DWI was trying to work out a plea deal with the County Attorney, so treatment was tied up in the court system.

I came home one afternoon to find Romeo trying to hook up an air compressor to his breathalyzer to see if he could circumvent the system. I did not say a word. Two weeks later, I came home to find him sitting in the garage drinking a Coors Light. My heart stopped.

I asked, "What are you doing?"

"I can drink now," he said laughing. "I sold a few things and posted an unconditional bail, so I do not need to be on the breathalyzer and have no other restrictions from the court until I go to trial this fall."

More unaccounted for cash Romeo had somehow come up with. Sadly, it was almost a relief because now he would be safer to live with since he could drink again. He also informed me that he was going to be taking on some side jobs to rebuild my savings account that had been drained once again covering his attorney fees for the DWI and Brynlee's custody case. He went on to say that he was going to have a friend from Minneapolis come down to help him with these side jobs and that he would be staying with us. I asked who and he told me a name that I did not like hearing. He was an old using friend of Romeos. I said, "No, you are not. I don't want him here near you, me, or Brynlee." Romeo became furious. I left and went to his moms. I asked her to call and talk to him about this. If both his mom and I were on him about what a bad idea this was, hopefully we could talk him out of it. However, by the time I got back home, this friend was already at the house. Fucking great.

The two of them started working from sunrise to sunset. Romeo was withdrawing from me and his mom. I was monitoring his behavior from the onset to look for signs of use. I was suspicious but could not be certain. He came home one night and told me he needed me to go sign some paperwork for a storage shed. I asked, "Why do you suddenly need a storage shed?" He became furious and started screaming at me to stop asking questions and not trusting him. He was acting extremely paranoid once again and told me that he had installed cameras and audio recording devices around the house because he didn't think that we could trust the neighbors anymore and also needed to make sure that I was not cheating on him when he was at work. I went out to our garage, and it was full of expensive tools that I had not seen before. He told me his friend had purchased them. I did not have a good feeling. I told him we could talk about it over the weekend. We had plans to go back to Minneapolis, and we had a lot of things we needed to discuss.

CHAPTER 5

ROMEO AND JULIET

I knew he was under the influence of something when we left home the next morning for our favorite fall motorcycle run. I thought if I could just get him away—doing what he loved most—then I could save him from yet another full relapse.

I had never harnessed the power to prevent him from relapsing, but this time seemed different. He was more shameful and honest, and there was also something else heavily weighing on him. I just didn't know what it was at the time.

So, I willingly packed up a few belongings and got on the back of a Harley with a man under the influence of drugs. It was not the first time that I had been on the back of a bike with Romeo while he was high, but it was the first time I was actually aware there had been some form of drug use.

In the days prior to leaving, he had been trying to find a way to tell me something. He would start and then stop.

"Babe, I really need to tell you something," he'd say as he paced around the house, which would get my attention, but only long enough for him to leave the room and completely shut down. He had also admitted to me two days before we left that someone at work had given him Ritalin. He had only admitted to snorting Ritalin a few times, but I had my suspicions that it was meth or at least cocaine, but, like always, I closed both eyes and did what Romeo wanted.

"I knew I shouldn't have snorted it," he said to me. "Because now I need meth." He said he had taken some that day, but he had flushed the rest away. There was something else far more serious that he still needed to tell me, but he did at least acknowledge some form of drug use.

We had been down this road before so many times, and I knew deep down he had already relapsed back to meth. Meth at times acted as a truth serum for Romeo. He was so out of his mind that he could no longer keep all of his lies straight, so he didn't even bother trying. But at the time, I convinced myself it had only been Ritalin like he had said and that he had only snorted it for two days, so there was a chance that I could save him from yet another spiral of complete self-destruction. We just needed to get away. I believed that there was hope because it was the very first time that he had ever admitted to me that he had used any kind of drug and more importantly expressly stated that he did not want to be going down that road again because he was scared about what could happen this time. There was also a dark, deep emotional sadness to Romeo, a side of him that I had never seen before. There was just something so very different about him this time, and not in a good way.

All the prior relapses started the same general way. He would eventually collapse from the vice grip he had over his addiction, make a phone call, tell me he was running to the store, and then disappear for days until he eventually would call and ask me to help him.

I also thought that the two of us getting away and having time together would allow him to open up about what he had been trying so hard to tell me for the past week. Maybe, just maybe, this time would be different. Romeo was in his own way crying out for help to me for the first time.

As we were on our way down to Minneapolis, he stopped a couple of times and kept making eerily sad references to the fact he really shouldn't be going on this bike run. I struggled trying to figure out why he would be saying that. It was like he knew something I didn't and wanted to prevent it from happening. In all of our years together, Romeo never once said he didn't feel like riding. Not one time. So, I kept encouraging him that this would be good for him— for us—to clear the air and get the two days of drug use out of his system. This was the earliest that I had picked up on a relapse and the very first time that Romeo actually admitted it and had stayed with me, rather than just disappearing into the night on a full-fledged relapse. I expressed how proud I was of him for being more open than normal about his looming relapse and reassured him that we would get through it together just like we always somehow found a way to stick together.

As I look back now, I realize that this was a really troubling indicator that something psychologically was really wrong with Romeo. Despite his addiction and mental health issues, he always had riding. Riding motorcycles was therapy for him. It cleared his head, and he could find peace within himself—two things he rarely was ever able to experience in life. I could watch the tension in his body relax, and his eyes showed less pain behind them. He would often share how good he felt after even a short ride; riding allowed him to separate from the demons he was always desperately fighting in his head.

This particular weekend, I thought this bike trip would help him clear his mind of what had been weighing him down and get him to tell me what was going on. Yet, that wasn't the case, nor would it ever be, considering the many betrayals he inflicted upon me, one of which I only found out after our bike trip. Romeo had cheated on me with a one-night fling and had gotten the woman pregnant. He knew I would leave him when I found out, and his life as he had known it would be over.

When we checked into the hotel where we were staying for the first night, he was isolating and agitated. He was not socializing like normal with friends who were staying at the same hotel, and he was very preoccupied with his phone. He paced around the room and then would run outside to take a phone call. I could hear his voice escalating to whomever he was talking to.

Out of nowhere, he told me he had something he needed to take care of and that he would be back in a little while.

"I won't be gone long," he said.

"But where are you going that's so important? Why can't I just come with you?" I asked, confused, even though deep down I knew exactly why he didn't want me coming with him.

Something was up. It either had to do with what had been preoccupying his mind, or he had no ability or intention to make his recent slip "just a slip" after all, and he was off to score drugs—or both. I was beginning to accept into my reality that he had not relapsed with Ritalin like he claimed before we left. He had already resumed using meth.

I spent the whole time he was gone frantically worrying about where he was, what he was doing, and if he was even going to come back at all. When the drugs were calling his name, Romeo heard nothing else. He became a robot, fixated on what he wanted at the expense of everything and everyone else. I sat on the bed with knots in my stomach replaying all his behaviors and words over the past couple of days. He returned about two hours later and was angry but didn't say much. I assumed he was unable to get what he wanted. I went to bed while he lay next to me buried in his phone. I didn't sleep much, and he didn't sleep at all. The ride was starting early the next day.

In the morning as I was getting ready, he said he was going to fill up on gas, grab a few things, and be right back. I was nervous the whole time he was gone. Why wouldn't we just get gas on our way like we normally would do? Why was it taking him so long when a gas station was a mile from the hotel? He came back about 45 minutes later in a much better mood. I tried to get a look at his eyes as his eyes always gave a clear indication if he had just used, but he had his sunglasses on and didn't take them off even when he came into the hotel room. He was in an extreme rush to get going. I was surprised at the fact that he didn't seem concerned about his appearance.

Romeo was always obsessed about how he looked, especially on the Harley. He had a very distinct riding style and always put a great deal of effort into matching his bandana with just the right Harley shirt, and on a cool morning like this, he would normally be wearing his leather chaps. It would always take him twice as long to get ready for a day riding than it would me. But not this day; he wore the same exact clothes as the day before, threw his belongings in the saddlebag, and yelled at me to hurry up. Something was wrong, very wrong.

As we began riding, he started asking really strange questions and kept isolating us away from the run route and our friends that we would normally socialize with.

"Why do you love me?" he asked.

"I love you because butterflies dance in my soul whenever you look me in the eyes or touch my skin. Even after everything we have been through, you still give me butterflies, just like the very first night we met at Neumann's Bar."

"What if I suddenly died? Would you find someone else?" he asked.

I told him to stop talking like that. "Nothing is going to happen to you, and no, I would never be able to love anyone like I love you. It is simply not possible, and you know that," I replied.

He told me he didn't believe me. I asked him to turn on the radio. Typically, we had the stereo thumping loud when we rode, but not that day. We just rode in silence. He was not connected to the bike or to me. He was mentally somewhere else, and it wasn't a good place.

We mysteriously stopped frequently for "bathroom" breaks at gas stations and isolated areas away from the bike run route and skipped many of the scheduled bar stops. This was not normal. The best part of a motorcycle run is the energy of riding in a large group and then socializing at the designated stops. There was a big party planned at the last stop, which we obviously had planned on attending as one of our favorite local bands was playing.

Romeo kept disappearing alone whenever we stopped and was then in a rush to get to the next stop. He was manic and disheveled. I consciously knew he had been using meth throughout the day, but I was in denial—the way I was always in denial about what was really happening. He was becoming more and more emotional, which was very out of the ordinary for him, especially when using. Drugs, especially meth, instantly hardened him and left him emotionally void, but not that day. In the first few days of a relapse, it is very hard to ascertain whether there has been actual use because when an addict is vice gripping against their addiction, they exhibit all the behaviors of actual use; at least Romeo did.

I knew I would be able to tell that night because if he had been using meth, the extreme paranoia would come out, and, of course, he wouldn't be able to sleep.

We had plans to stay at a hotel in a small town that night near where the motorcycle ride ended. Romeo kept telling me he wanted to cut the run short and get to the hotel. This was also very strange behavior for him.

"Can we please stop so I can get something to eat?" I asked.

"No, let's get to the hotel."

I kept asking him why he was in such a rush to get to the hotel. We had not eaten all day.

"Aren't we going to the party tonight?" I inquired.

"I changed my mind," he curtly replied. "I don't feel like being around other people, and you don't need to be around anyone else. You have been talking and flirting with way too many people already today."

After much deliberation, I was able to get him to stop so that I could eat. He couldn't sit still and refused to order anything, telling me to hurry up. His mom called twice while I was eating, but he didn't take her call. This was odd because he always took his mom's call, and Brynlee was staying with her while we were gone. I asked why he wasn't answering, and he started crying and mumbling about how he was tired of people wanting to talk to him and other really strange, out-of-context things.

"I'm fucking tired of people making demands on me," he said.

"Are you talking about work?" I inquired. "Your mom? Brynlee's custody case? What are you talking about?"

"Just shut the fuck up," he said. "I just need everyone to be quiet, especially you."

I just could not figure out where all these emotions were coming from. This was such abnormal behavior when he was using. He would become extremely paranoid, manic, and violent, but not emotional and most certainly not to the point of crying, let alone in public. I had learned how to "manage" his anger and paranoia, but not this bizarre sadness and complete despair.

I explained that his mom and daughter were not "people"; they were family. His mom then called my phone. He forcefully grabbed my phone, shoved it into his pocket, and said, "Just leave it alone."

It was then that I finally got a good look into his eyes and knew he was under the influence of meth. His eyes were dilated and wild. He was hollow and empty inside. He immediately broke eye contact and quickly put his sunglasses on. When clean, Romeo and I had a deeply powerful connection when our eyes locked. It had been that way since the very first moment we met and looked at each other across a crowded room. I could calm him, and we both expressed love to each other by merely looking into each other's eyes. Our eyes spoke more words than most people's voices ever could.

I was getting angry. "What is wrong with you?" I asked. "Let's just check in with them and make sure everything is okay. You know your mom; she is going to keep calling until one of us answers, so I am going to check in with her."

That's when he jumped up, grabbed my arm, threw cash down on the bar, and said, "We are leaving now."

At this point, I just wanted to get to the hotel so I could figure out what in the hell was going on and separate myself from him. I actually believed he would just drop me off and then leave to go find his using friends. That had happened more times than I could count over the course of our relationship. I had already been making plans in my head of who I could call to come pick me up because something was not right, and I had a really sick feeling in my stomach.

On the way to the hotel, he didn't speak a word. We just rode in the same eerie silence we had all day until we approached a bridge that crossed a river, and he suddenly took both hands off the motorcycle.

"What if we would just drift off the road and into the water? People would think it was just an accident."

Silent and unsure how to respond, I was scared. He was coming undone in a way that I had not ever seen before. After all the years and all the relapses, I truly thought I had lived it all with him. I knew better than to start yelling at him, so I tried to start talking to him about random things about his daughters and how good it would feel to get to the hotel and have a beer.

"A cold one will taste so good when we get back, huh, babe?" I said. "I can't wait to get to the hotel with you."

Romeo glanced back at me on the bike and said, "I just want to relax, really relax. You want to relax with me, babe, right? You really love me, right?"

While it was only about a 15-mile drive to the hotel, it seemed like we rode forever. Romeo parked in front of the lobby door and told me to get us checked in. I assumed he would be gathering our stuff off the bike, but when I came back, he was just standing in the same spot watching my every move.

"Did you see anyone you know in there?" he asked.

"No, why would you ask me that?"

There was a long pause before he said, "Give me the key."

I handed him the hotel room key and started to take out the beers and our personal belongings from the saddlebags on the bike while he just bolted into the hotel room. When I got into the room, I watched as he walked into the bathroom without closing the door. I saw him pull a bubble out of his pocket and smoke meth right in front of me.

"What the fuck are you doing?" I asked.

"Nothing," he said.

"Is that meth?"

"Yes," he sat matter-of-factly.

I got up and started going through my purse looking for my phone but then remembered that it was still in his pocket. He became increasingly agitated. He deadbolted the door, closed the blinds on the windows, and pulled my phone out of his pocket.

"Is this what you're looking for?" he asked me.

I played dumb and said no. "I have a headache and was just looking for something to take for it," I lied.

"Relax. It's time for a beer, babe," he said, handing me a can without opening one for himself.

"They're warm. Put them in the fridge," I demanded, then wondered why he wasn't cleaning up after the ride like he normally would.

"Aren't you going to shower?"

He didn't answer. He just put my beer on the nightstand. Also very odd. Romeo always had a beer in his hand.

"Come sit down with me," he said as he lay down on the bed.

That's when he picked up my cell phone again and slowly started going through each and every one of my contacts. He scrolled around, picking out names of people he knew were colleagues of mine from years ago or clients or an ex from the past that he crazily believed I still wanted to be with.

"You'll end up with one of them if something happens to me," Romeo said. "You probably already know who and can't wait to be with him."

He then put my phone back in his pocket and started Googling booty bumping on his own phone. I knew what booty bumping was because he had explained it to me in the past, as it was one of his favorite ways to use meth for a quick and powerful high.

"People really like it," he said. "It really gets them off. You might like it."

"I know what it is," I replied. "Why would you possibly think I would like it or ever do it? What is wrong with you?"

"Listen, babe, people who don't even use love having sex on it. It is better than ecstasy. You need to start loosening up. I think it is just what we need to spice up our sex life. You want to make me happy, don't you? Just read about it," he said as he was aggressively shoving his phone to my face.

I kept trying to ignore him and change the subject. He suddenly went into the bathroom and came out a few minutes later with a Mountain Dew bottle. "It's time, babe."

He walked over to me on the bed.

"What are you doing?" I asked. "Where did that come from? Why are you shaking it, and what is in it?"

"Water. Meth."

"What? No, I'm not doing that." My voice was shaking.

"I am going to booty bump you and then we will make love like crazy, and it will be amazing. I promise, babe. I love you so much."

He started crying again. He had cried more in the past 24 hours than he had in all the years we had been together. He then proceeded to roll me over onto the bed, turn me on my stomach, and forcefully inserted the bottle into my asshole. The contents of the bottle emptied deep inside me.

Within just a few minutes, I felt the back of my head go numb, and my heart started racing. I began running circles around the hotel room. Romeo lay calmly on the bed.

"Don't worry. It'll be over soon," he said.

The first thought I had was that he was going to kill us both. Just like in the famous Shakespearean love story where the characters Romeo and Juliet tragically end up both committing suicide because neither could bear the thought of living without the other. He had told me so many times over the years that he wanted to die, but was scared of dying alone. And that he knew he could not do it, because he was not going to leave me because I would just end up with some other man. I remember thinking he had actually reached the point where he could not live any longer, and out of some sort of twisted love for me, my Romeo was about to end both of our lives in that hotel room. But that was just more of my delusional thinking.

I became increasingly panicked—manic. Everything in my body seemed not to be working the way it should, and I suddenly realized that I was going to die.

"You're going to kill us, aren't you?" I asked. "You're going to kill us both!"

He just peacefully lay there and said again to just relax.

"It'll be over soon," he said.

I started screaming. "I'm not ready to die!"

I still had things that I needed to do. Things I wanted to do. People to see and love and places to go and explore. A life to live. At no point did Romeo ever try to comfort me, make any attempt whatsoever to have sex with me, or even touch me. Instead, he was deeply enjoying watching me unravel.

"Babe, you're just being paranoid," he said. "From the drugs."

He calmly sat on the bed smoking meth and watching me. I believed with every fiber of my being that I was going to die. I had passing thoughts of lucidity where I couldn't understand why he was so calm and why I was becoming more and more manic.

I clearly understand now that he had no intention of romantically reenacting the ending scene of "Romeo and Juliet." It was only me that was going to die as he peacefully watched me no longer become an obstacle in his life. I became completely hysterical as images of everything I'd done in my life flashed before me—all the things that I had still not done and all the wrongs that I needed to make right before I left this earth.

As time went on—how long I don't know—Romeo became very concerned that I was still manic.

"Why the fuck won't you just calm down?" he yelled at me. "Just calm the fuck down."

He shoved me in the bathroom and started telling me that if I didn't shut the fuck up that someone was going to call the police.

"You don't want that because you're high as a kite, and you'll go to jail or a psych ward because you're being a crazy bitch," he said.

He suddenly started pacing around the hotel. "It wasn't supposed to go like this."

"Like what!" I screamed.

"Nothing. But if you calm down, we can go for a little ride on the bike. How about that? Would you like that, babe? I think that is what we need to do now. It will calm you down."

"Fuck, fuck, it wasn't supposed to take this long," he kept repeating. "What am I going to do now? How am I going to get this dumb bitch on the bike?"

I don't know how much time went by from when he booty bumped me to when I collapsed on the floor in front of the bed and finally started breathing normally. I remember taking my first full breaths of air and looking up to see Romeo standing by the hotel door like he was ready to bolt out at any moment. He was just staring at me and waiting to see what I was going to do or say. Time just kept passing.

It was morning, and a whole night had passed. I felt more coherent but obviously in shock and significantly still under the influence. I remember looking up at him and feeling this overwhelming sense to protect myself.

Although I was lucid, I played dumb.

"What happened?" I muttered. "What's going on?"

He looked surprised that I didn't start screaming or accusing him of anything. I acted confused as if I was trying to figure out what happened.

"Don't know what's wrong with you," he said.

I knew instantly my only way out was to play along with him. It was working.

He asked what was wrong with me—now he was playing dumb. He had left all his personal belongings on the bed, getting ready to leave with nothing but the clothes on his back.

"Only thing I remember is you giving me that beer." I pointed to the bedside table where my unopened can of beer still sat. "What happened?"

"You went crazy. No reason really, but you got some issues."

"What kind of issues?" I asked.

"I don't know. Serious ones, though."

"Like what? Tell me!"

I tried to keep him talking as I looked around the hotel. The hotel phone was now missing from the table, and I assumed he still had my cell. I was not feeling well, my ears were ringing, my vision was impaired, and my body was trembling. My heart was pounding, and it was hard to take breaths. My mind raced.

I wanted the fuck out of that hotel room.

I started to pack up my things, pretending I was paranoid from the drugs and not showing what I was really doing—plotting my escape.

He was watching my every move. Why did he stay in the hotel? Why didn't he just leave? Not having the capacity to even link one thought to the next, I told him we needed to get out of the hotel. I could see him just standing by the door, tears pouring down his face.

Then the drugs got a hold of me again. I had the urge to start walking around in circles and felt like the walls of the hotel room were caving in on me. I knew he was paranoid, so I continued to use that to my advantage. I went to the window and told him a cop car had just driven through the parking lot.

"I wonder if they're here for us," I said.

He started to panic. "Get your shit together. We are leaving. You sure you saw a cop?"

"But I'm sick," I said. "I want to call Sara." I made up my mind that I would call my girlfriend and have her come pick me up. I knew as soon as Romeo left the hotel, I could get to a phone.

"You sure you saw a cop out there?" he repeated. "We are staying together; I don't care how you are feeling. You are not going anywhere without me."

"Yeah, babe. There was a cop standing right by our bike. He just stood there. You better get out of here."

I could almost see the wheels turning in his head. He wanted out of the hotel; he was paranoid about the police but also didn't want to leave me alone.

"What if the cop wrote down the license plate?" I was playing him good now, especially since Romeo did not have a valid driver's license at that time. If he were to be stopped for any reason, he'd be arrested on the spot. "You better not get on the bike." Why don't you just call Joe and get out of here right now? I will take a shower and call you in a little while to see where you are."

"Fuck, okay. I'm calling Joe, but you are coming with me, guaranteed." He agreed to call his one and only friend to pick us up in his truck and trailer the bike to Minneapolis. I knew if I could just get to Minneapolis, I could call Sara for help.

Joe finally arrived. He helped Romeo secure the bike on the trailer, and the three of us jumped into the truck. Romeo was really, really anxious on the short drive and had tears in his eyes. I am sure he was scared that I was going to say something to his friend about what happened the night before, but I did not. I was barely holding myself together and considering this was a friend of his that he had met in prison, I did not feel safe saying anything about what had happened.

"Do you still have my phone?" I asked.

"No," he lied. I could see it poking out of his pocket.

I made light of his lying and played more of my little game. My little game that was saving my life.

"Oh, babe. I see it in your pocket. Just give it here. I need to charge the battery," I said.

Not wanting to make a scene in front of his friend, Romeo reluctantly handed me my phone. I still had battery power left, so I put the phone in my back pocket.

As soon as we hit the outskirts of Minneapolis, I told his friend that I needed to go to the bathroom and to take the next exit. I told Romeo there was a large parking lot at the gas station so he could get the bike unloaded from the trailer while I went to the bathroom. Romeo was not happy, but also not wanting to make waves with his friend, who was in a rush to get somewhere and not overly thrilled about having to pick us up early on a Sunday morning, agreed that we could take the exit. I immediately bolted from the vehicle and ran into the nearest building—a hotel—and hid. I could hear Romeo get on the motorcycle and drive through the parking lot over and over again looking for me. I waited and waited until I could no longer see or hear the rumble of the bike.

After an hour of not hearing the bike or Romeo calling me, I felt safe enough to get help. I called Sara, who came and picked me up. I told her nothing about what happened, just that Romeo and I had a fight and I needed to get back home. She asked me if I wanted to talk about it, and I said I couldn't. She just gave me space and turned up the radio. Thank God for friends like Sara.

I don't even really remember much about that drive. I know I just sat, clenching my backpack, trying to process what happened. I had waves of feeling normal and then waves of my heart racing.

Sara drove me part way from Minneapolis so that I could meet Romeo's mom, who picked me up at a gas station to bring me the rest of the way home. I got into her vehicle, and she asked, "What happened? Where's Romeo?"

I began crying hysterically. "He relapsed and something really bad happened this time, really bad, and I don't know where he is," I responded.

I was not in the mental space that I could even think about telling Romeo's mom about what happened in that hotel room. I just wanted to be alone and try to process things myself. She asked nothing further, dropped me off at home, and said she would call me in the morning. She was all too used to the secrets and lies of our relationship.

I finally made it inside the house. I had no idea where Romeo was, but assumed that he was still in Minneapolis with his old drug using friends. I knew the last place he would come was back home that night because he knew I would be in contact with his mom and Ellie.

I decided to try to sleep and then sort through what to do next in the morning. Obviously, still being heavily under the influence of meth, I could not sleep. I just lay in bed, mind racing, trying to piece together what happened. *Had he tried to kill just me or both of us? If not that, why didn't he help me? Why didn't he comfort me? Why did he keep saying it wasn't supposed to happen like this? Why didn't he just leave the hotel room? He had to have planned to also take his own life, right? Where was he now? What was he going to do next? When was he going to come back to the house?*

As I replayed the events over and over in my head, I suddenly couldn't catch my breath. I got up and walked into the bathroom, but it was becoming harder and harder to catch my breath. I tried to drink a glass of water but couldn't. I suddenly felt sharp pains in my lower back, and I started bleeding out of my ass. I was hyperventilating and thought, *Okay, now I really am dying.*

I collapsed on the floor but had enough wherewithal to call 911.

It seemed like forever for them to get there, but eventually I heard sirens, police, an ambulance, and other vehicles. They entered my house and found me. One of the paramedics was the guy who owned the little grocery store in town. Someone else was a mutual friend that Romeo and I saw all of the time. Everyone was asking me questions: "Where is Romeo? What happened? What did Romeo do to you this time? Did I know of any reason why I may be bleeding out of my ass?"

Fucking great. Now I had to tell the single most embarrassing story to humans I knew. However, I didn't tell them what he actually did. I lied, just like I always did.

"I let him booty bump me," I lied. "I let him do it." I was scared and humiliated. I only knew how to protect Romeo, not how to protect myself from him.

The police didn't believe me. The look on the paramedic's face in the ambulance was of sheer and utter disbelief and one that I will never forget.

"What kind of fucked up man does something like that?" The medic wasn't buying my story and urged me to tell the truth as we rode to the emergency room. "You need to tell the truth. You're in danger. He is going to kill you next time."

I just wanted to close my eyes and sleep. I wanted silence and for everyone to go away and for my mind to shut off.

I awoke the next morning to a doctor standing over me in the hospital room, telling me that I needed to wake up, as there were officers who needed to talk to me. I just kept my eyes tightly closed, thinking if I did that long enough, everyone would just leave.

I couldn't form thoughts. I felt sick and confused and completely overwhelmed. I just wanted to die. As I went over in my mind the facts of what had happened over the past 48 hours, tears poured down my face, and the police started asking me so many questions.

"Where is he?" they asked.

"I don't know," I replied.

"When did you last have contact with him?"

"I don't know." It was the only answer I had in me for the next 20 questions coming my way.

"Did he force you to do something you did not want to do?"

"I don't know."

"Where were you when he gave you the drugs?"

"I don't know."

"How long has it been since he gave you the drugs?"

"I don't know."

"Do you have a safe place to go?"

"I don't know."

They eventually left and told me to get some rest and that someone would be by later to talk to me again. They gave me a card to the local domestic abuse center and continued on endlessly about the fact I needed to immediately obtain an order for protection against Romeo. Too ashamed to reach out to my friends and not wanting to deal with Romeo's mom about why I called 911, I walked out of the hospital in my pajamas with no shoes and called a cab for a ride home.

I walked into my house and looked around to see if Romeo had been back; he had not. I looked at my phone, and he called all throughout the night and morning. I sat down on the couch, as it was Monday and I needed to work. I couldn't even pull myself together enough to remember my passwords to log in to my computer. I started panicking, and my heart was racing. I took whatever medication the doctor had given me and was able to sleep for a couple of hours. Romeo was blowing up my phone, so I finally answered.

"Why didn't you answer?" he screamed.

"I was in the hospital," I said.

"Why were you in the hospital? What that fuck did you tell them?"

"Tell who?" I asked.

"The cops! Don't play dumb with me, bitch!"

I just hung up the phone, took a few more pills, and slept for quite some time. I woke up to a pounding headache, seeing black spots, and had a constant ringing in my ears. I knew I had to work and deal with all the messages from friends, neighbors, the police, and, of course, Romeo. I started giving everyone the same very watered down, untruthful version of what happened.

"We were on a motorcycle trip, he did something to me, and I am not talking about it," I said.

I was still barely functioning when Romeo called two days later just as another set of officers were backing out of our driveway. He was in the throes of use, angry at me and untrusting of anything that came out of my mouth. I avoided any discussions of the hotel night and instead told him how DEA agents had just been to the house to ask me questions about him and his friend regarding drugs and stolen property. I told him that the sheriff's office had found that storage shed he had rented the previous week. I also told him how his boss had been to the house, taken back the tools he had stolen, and filed a police report about other missing work equipment that I could not find at the house. Romeo had been very busy doing all kinds of things in the month before we had left on that ride. At one point, he became violently angry, telling me how if he had just given me a "little bit more," none of this would be happening.

"I should have given it all to you. You wouldn't be here, and I wouldn't be in this fucking mess. I am watching you, bitch, and I have people watching you. Bet that," he screamed.

It was in that conversation that I knew exactly what his intention had been that night, and it was nothing even close to the romantic Romeo and Juliet delusion that my mind had subconsciously created to help protect me from the truth. I wished with all my heart that I would have been brave enough to call the police and tell them everything, but I wasn't.

A week or two later, the sheriff's department was back at my house informing me that Romeo had now been charged with several counts of felony theft, among pending drug-related charges. Not only had he stolen from his employer, but he had been taking cash from local residents for down payments on construction jobs but never showed up to start the jobs. I now knew how he had suddenly been coming up with all that cash.

I told the officers that I believed he was in Minneapolis, and that was all I knew, but I would help them locate him any way I could.

Later that week, I received a phone call from my employer informing me that the legal department of the company I was working for was unexpectedly being relocated to Warsaw, Poland, and my position would be ending in a few weeks. *Fucking great.* I remember falling to the floor in my living room and crying for hours. Over the course of the next several weeks, Romeo remained on the run. At times, he would call crying and saying that he was coming home to get his things and face his charges.

"I need to face this," he'd say. "I will go to treatment this time," but by then he was out of lies I'd allow myself to believe. He was out of ways he could hurt me.

Other times, he just wanted to know if people were talking about him, if I had seen his kids, and what court papers had been sent to the house regarding his new criminal cases and a pending DWI case he had open from earlier in the year. In addition to everything else going on, I was also dealing with the County Attorney's office in another county for the Child in Need of Protective Services trial that was underway for Brynlee.

I continued to cooperate with the police to help find Romeo while looking for a new job out of the area and away from everything connected to him. He and I maintained ongoing phone contact. I came close a few times to pinpointing his whereabouts, but he was a skilled professional at evading both me and law enforcement. Sometimes he was so strung out I couldn't even understand him. At other times, he was crying and suicidal or violently angry and threatening. I know that at least a couple of times he was outside of our home because he would call to say, "Look out the living room window, babe. I am home. You better not have another man in my house." And I would see him in a vehicle on the street staring straight at our house. Fear and panic would shoot through every inch of my body. It was always a different car, and the sheriff's office could never make it out in time to catch him. I believe Romeo never came into the house because he did not trust me anymore and had convinced himself that I had been working with the police. He asked me on the phone more than once why there was a sheriff's car around the house so much and what I had been saying to them.

During one call, though, it felt like the final showdown in a movie, except this was real life, and I wasn't going to let him get one more try.

"I'm coming home. Get ready. Things are going to get ugly. I don't care who all dies tonight."

I could tell by the difficulty he was having breathing and the aggressiveness in his voice that he had been mixing drugs and was on a very bad trip.

"What are you talking about?"

"Come home and get your things," I said. "Take what you want."

"The only thing I want," Romeo said, "is for the world to go black. I am fucking tired of seeing red. It is all going to end tonight, and I don't care who I have to kill."

I immediately contacted 911, called the neighbors to warn them, got out of the house, and waited the night in a hotel for the police to call and tell me that they had arrested him. That did not happen. Romeo never came to the house. He called a few days later and had no recollection of that conversation.

Another month went by. In December of 2015, I found a corporate attorney position and relocated to Moorhead, Minnesota. Brynlee was eventually court ordered to live with her aunt and uncle, which is the best thing that could have happened to her as they were kind, loving people. While it was difficult for me to let go of all contact with her, it was what was best for all of us. Emma remained living with her mother and stepfather.

Romeo was still on the run, and we were maintaining some phone contact so that I could keep tabs on his whereabouts for the police and for my own safety. A couple of weeks later, I finally received a call from the police indicating that he had been arrested in Minneapolis on yet another new charge. I couldn't believe this was finally going to be over. With all the felony charges he had against him, he would eventually be going to prison for a long time, and I would never need to tell anyone what really happened in that hotel room. I could keep my shameful secret buried forever.

Little did I know that this was far from behind me. For a month, Romeo bounced from one county jail to another county jail dealing with all of his active warrants. By a gross error in judgment, a judge released him on nothing but a promise to appear pending all of his court appearances for his numerous cases. Upon his release, Romeo's mother told him that I had moved to Moorhead, Minnesota. In January of 2016, he came to find me, and within days of arriving, he was arrested for his second pending felony DWI and was jailed less than two miles from where I had just moved. I was confident that with this new felony charge he would remain incarcerated until all of his trials were completed and he was sentenced back to prison.

Once again, I was wrong, very wrong.

CHAPTER 6

TRAUMA HEALING

My first attempt at healing from the trauma of not only what happened the night in the hotel but all the other traumatic events and abuse throughout the entire relationship was very aggressive. I was angry at Romeo, myself, and the entire world. I lived in a rigid fight-response state and strong-armed myself into a perceived place of healing.

Identical to Romeo's attempt to vice grip his way to stay clean his entire adult life, I vice gripped my first attempt at healing. And, like anything you attempt to prevent, heal, or recover from by sheer willpower alone, you eventually fail.

It was obviously not without its benefits; any action of healing is better than no action. I went full force ahead at not only closing the circle of what happened with Romeo but barricading it with brick and mortar and then shouting from the hilltops that I won, and he lost. I was going to live my life just as if nothing had happened.

My vice gripping attempt at healing worked like this: I woke up, went to the gym, went to work, attended a weekly appointment with my trauma therapist, and spent the rest of the time at home with my dog, Maicy. Rinse and repeat for over a year. I was diagnosed with complex PTSD and put on medication along with my therapy to help ease the effects. As long as I stayed in the existence of this safety bubble, I convinced myself that I was healing. Now, mind you that throughout this entire time period, Romeo and I were in contact with each other via jail phone calls and jail visits. One reason was that I needed to keep track of his whereabouts while his various trials were underway. He was facing a very long prison sentence, and I knew that if he was somehow able to post bail again, he was going to go back on the run, and my life would be in danger.

And if I am being truly honest, another reason was that even after everything that happened, I was still having difficulty severing that toxic trauma bond that was so intricately woven into every fiber of my soul. A big part of me was also enjoying the fact that he was locked up and still actually thought there was a chance I was going to bail him out and take him back. It was the way I finally took back my power. It was my own sweet, secret little revenge, but very unhealthy. My therapist agreed keeping minimal telephone contact was appropriate for the purpose of keeping tabs on him until he was safely in prison, but that I needed to stop going to see him. I did not take her advice. I enjoyed listening to him beg me for a nominal amount of bail money as he sat behind yet another jail visitation window all the while knowing that nothing that he could say would ever let me feel safe around him again.

The single greatest takeaway from my first attempt at healing was this: There was no way to effectively heal from abuse and trauma while still maintaining the contact I had with Romeo. When you are in a toxic relationship, a dangerous subconscious coping mechanism automatically occurs whereby you disconnect from your wise self and romanticize the person and events because acknowledging the truth of your reality is impossible for your psyche to comprehend. This disconnection is called dissociation. Dissociation is the subconscious process in which your mind so elegantly dances away from the reality of your life and carries you to a place of perceived reality. The unconscious mind does this when the pain and fear of what is really going on is too much for the conscious mind to process. You start convincing yourself that the person is different from who they really are, and you have a justification for all of their behaviors because doing this is easier and requires less strength than accepting what is really going on. It was easier for me to keep trying to convince myself that it was somehow okay what Romeo did because he was under the influence of drugs when he did it. My thought process was focused on how I could justify his behavior rather than seeing it for what it was: *Romeo was not a monster the night he slammed my head repeatedly into the cement floor of our garage because he was hearing voices telling him that I was someone else; it was his mental illness and drug addiction causing it, so I better just love him more and try harder to get him the help he needs.* You also take an ordinary act or strange behavior and romanticize it into a fictitious act of love. *Romeo's act of installing cameras inside and outside every inch of our home was done because he loved the girls and I so much he wanted to keep us safe from the unsavory people he brought into our lives, not because of his dangerous paranoia and drug addiction.*

Rinse and repeat over years, and trust me when I say you lose all ability to differentiate what is real from what your mind concocted to protect you. You become detached from yourself and your life. You become numb and robotic. Recognizing and dealing with dissociation is the single biggest roadblock to getting out of toxic relationships and healing from trauma. In so many cases, you do not realize how much danger you are in until it is too late. I was lucky. The universe intervened and finally separated me and Romeo because, clearly, I was unable to protect myself.

I was still not facing the reality of what my entire relationship with Romeo was like, abusive and toxic. I had also become toxic, and it was standing in the way of any real healing. Parts of me believed that I still loved him very much, but the thought of him ever getting back out of jail or being around him alone terrified me to my core. It was yet another cognitive dissonance that I needed to face and heal. Cognitive dissonance occurs when your thoughts and behaviors are not aligned with the reality of your circumstances. It's holding two completely different beliefs at the exact same time. I am scared of him, but I love him. I hate him, but I love him. He hurts me, but I love him. He tried to kill me, but I love him. I know I can never be with him again, but I still love him.

Now, over two years after the event in the hotel and a year of intense trauma counseling, a part of my psyche was still convinced that what happened in that hotel room was the ultimate act of love, a true Romeo and Juliet love tragedy. Romeo did not want to live anymore but couldn't bear to leave me, so he was going to end both of our lives. However, that was not the truth. The truth was that the man I loved more than anyone or anything in the world had attempted to take only my life, and there was nothing fucking romantic about that. There would have been no other plausible reason that he did what he did and said what he said. I needed to accept this into my reality, or I was never going to be able to start healing.

Romanticizing and missing a relationship that was abusive is a trauma bond, not love. Trauma bonds are created subconsciously and are very dangerous. They are what keep women in abusive relationships. Freeing yourself from the hold of a trauma bond is a very difficult process to go through and was the single most challenging aspect of my healing journey. When I say that I had become addicted to Romeo, I mean that I was physically, emotionally, and psychologically unable to separate myself from him. Clearly the fact that I was still voluntarily having contact with him while he was in jail is testament to the complete mental control abusers have over their victims. Think about that; really think about that. It should make you shudder in disbelief, but it is the truth. Even after everything that happened, I still could not let that man go. A trauma bond is an indescribably powerful hold and an addiction itself. The frightening part is that you are not able to recognize that one has formed until you are out of the relationship. And many abused women will never have the privilege to discover it before it is too late.

For every woman who has lost their life to domestic violence, I know that there was a powerful trauma bond in place. The key to educating women on how to leave abusive relationships is to get them to recognize this bond and break it. What I find very frustrating is that not once in three years of my intense trauma therapy did either of my therapists ever mention a trauma bond. It was only after a friend questioned me about how and why I was still "in love" with Romeo that I started getting really curious about why I was still in love with him. I started researching every possible explanation for how it was that I still missed him, that I still obsessed about the "good times," that I thought about him all the time, that I was still justifying his behavior, even what happened in that hotel room, when from the beginning, the relationship was clearly abusive and dangerous. It was through this self-taught work that I discovered that I still had a very powerful trauma bond to Romeo. I then started to learn how to dissolve that bond and free myself from its suffocating and blinding hold.

Much to my surprise, in the summer of 2016, I received a phone call from a local attorney asking me what my relationship was with Romeo. He was contacting me because Romeo (a perfected con artist) had made "friends" with a mentally challenged man in county jail who had a power of attorney overseeing his large trust fund while he was temporarily incarcerated. The attorney who called me was this power of attorney serving over the management of his financial affairs. Somehow, Romeo had convinced this mentally challenged man to post his bail via his power of attorney. I informed this attorney that he was very dangerous, unstable, and was facing a very long prison sentence. The attorney said he felt very uncomfortable with this request from his client and that he had been advising his client against it for days. Ultimately, the attorney had to do what his client was telling him to do. I begged him to delay the paperwork for a day because I needed to make an emergency move before bail was posted. So, within 48 hours, I made arrangements with my landlord to break my rental lease and relocate from Moorhead, Minnesota, to Fargo, North Dakota. With the assistance of friends and the protection of law enforcement, I was able to move about one hour before he was released from jail on bail. He shortly thereafter entered a long-term in-patient treatment program in hopes of receiving a reduced prison sentence.

Romeo was eventually sentenced to prison for a multitude of offenses (none of which included what happened in that hotel room because I was never brave enough to tell the truth). All communication between us finally ceased, and I started stepping out of my safety bubble and into living life more freely. I started to learn what safety felt like, and it was liberating. For so many years, I believed that I would never feel safe again. I started dating again, going out, building friendships, and trying to put the past behind me.

But I was tired of working on myself. I just wanted to be "normal" again, even though I had no idea what that really meant. It was at this time that I started feeling the overwhelmingly strong calling from the Universe to share my relationship with Romeo with the world so that I could help others in the same or similar situations. As this calling became stronger, I embarked on the powerful journey of my second attempt at healing, healing that was deep and authentic and that required me to own my story of what happened, all of what happened. You cannot heal if you are pretending you are not wounded. I kept remembering those moments in the hotel room where my life was flashing before my eyes of all the undone things in my life, and I started completing those undone circles. The more of those little circles that I closed, the more space I created for healing to enter the deep cracks in my soul.

This round of healing was softer, an intricate soul dance between grit and grace where I allowed acceptance and forgiveness into my reserve of necessary healing tools. True forgiveness is a slow process of letting go; to forgive is to learn how to detach yourself from that which you cannot change. I forgave Romeo; but more importantly, I forgave myself for thinking that it was love, for taking him back over and over, for being terrified, for being stuck, for protecting him, for lying for him, for losing myself, and for remaining a victim for as long as I did. You also cannot heal if you are still being a victim of your circumstances, even when the circumstances were not your fault.

While there is no quick fix to trauma healing, I firmly believe that there is a foundational framework that trauma survivors need to put in place to be able to move forward and free themselves from the effects of trauma. I view this process like putting together a jigsaw puzzle. It is much easier to complete a puzzle if you start with the frame. The pieces to the frame of your puzzle may be slightly different than my pieces, and you may put that frame together in a different order, but the following are pieces that I found are required for healing as effectively as possible:

1. Detach completely from the individual (unless you are tied to that person with kids, etc., and if this is your situation, put safety measures in place).
2. Feel, and I mean deeply feel, everything about what you are experiencing or have experienced.
3. Identify and address any underlying mental health or addiction issues you may have, and seek professional help.
4. Eat healthy foods, reduce or remove alcohol from your life, and exercise daily.
5. Spend time alone healing before you get into another relationship.
6. Identify what was missing from your life when you allowed an abusive person in. What voids were you not filling yourself that caused you to settle for a toxic relationship?

7. Build healthy female friendships if you are a woman or healthy male relationships if you are a man.
8. Be of service to your community. All victims of domestic abuse end up isolated, and learning to feel connected is a critical step to healing.
9. Find a spiritual or religious practice that provides you with support and guidance.
10. Acknowledge what happened to you, all of what happened to you. Own every single word of your story.
11. Forgive your abuser.
12. And forgive yourself.

View this list as ongoing self-care. As time goes on, it will no longer feel like a list that you need to check off; rather, it will become a way of living and showing up in the world. Live life as an alchemist; constantly be evaluating what is working and not working in your life. Take out what is not working, and put in what you need. There will be a lot of trial and error in this process, and that is okay. The most important of all the pieces is forgiveness— forgiveness of the person who hurt you, but far more importantly, forgiveness of yourself. Forgiveness is the only path to ensuring that no single person or event will ever hold power over you again.

I often asked myself what held me hostage to fear—both the fear I had of Romeo and, later, the fear I had around getting honest about all that I had experienced. The answer was shame. One cannot talk about healing from domestic violence without addressing shame. Of all the emotions that I noticed from all the women I professionally represented over all those years, shame was the most predominant. Every single woman felt embarrassed to be in the situation she was in. Why is that? I was no different. Of all the emotions I had, shame was also the one I most strongly identified with. I have never been more embarrassed of anything than my relationship with Romeo. I was embarrassed that I allowed someone to treat me the way I allowed Romeo to treat me. I was embarrassed that I gave away my power as a woman to the extent that I almost allowed another human being to take my life. I felt more shame for myself than I did anger at Romeo, and that is what happens in abusive relationships.

As women and as a collective community of domestic abuse survivors, we need to remove the shame associated with the relationship(s) we found ourselves in. We start to remove the shame by owning and sharing our stories with each other and the world. Isolation engulfs domestic abuse victims, and the only way to break through that isolation is to speak up. I did not speak up when I had the chance to tell the police what really happened in that hotel room, and now I have to live with that choice for the rest of my life. Do not follow my lead on that. Speak up and do not allow dangerous abusers like Romeo to walk away from what they did. I just pray that no other woman loses her life because of my inability to tell the truth. Yes, I was absolutely afraid of what may have happened to me if I did. Romeo had a lot of connections to some very dangerous people. However, the truth is I also chose to protect him because of how embarrassed I was over the details of what happened in that hotel. Shame hides us in a false sense of security, while truth sets us free. I hid under the unique safety net that I had because I already knew he was going back to prison. So, I convinced myself that it was okay to lie about what happened because Romeo wasn't going to be able to hurt anyone else.

In 2019, this guilt all came crashing down on me when I discovered that, due to a legal loophole in his sentencing, Romeo would be eligible for early release and back out on the streets on supervised parole after serving only a fraction of his sentence. I continue to pray that in the treatment program he went through before prison, he received the help he desperately needed for his addiction and mental health issues so that he is now able to live a drug and violence-free life—for everyone's safety. Be brave and choose truth, as it is not only the right thing to do, it will allow for a much quicker path of healing than I had.

Through the second attempt at healing, I forced myself to live in the reality of the truth of what happened to me, my role in the relationship, and my responsibility for growing through the experience into a better version of myself—PTSD and all. You truly take your power back when you take full ownership of your life. While I did not in any way deserve what happened to me that night in the hotel or all the years of abuse, I did need to take responsibility for the fact I should never have gotten involved with Romeo in the first place, let alone stayed in that dangerous relationship for as long as

I did. And, I definitely should not have let shame and fear prevent me from telling the truth when I made that 911 call. The irony of the most significant lesson I learned was that some life experiences are not meant or even possible to close and tuck away. Rather, peace and true healing can only be found in the equilibrium of owning what happened to you and learning to live your best life alongside of the pain and residual side effects of the experience. You must be able to see your own footprints in the ashes of the life situations you find yourself in.

There are some things that happen in life that you cannot heal from completely. Sometimes lives are broken so violently, and the pieces are so shattered that they cannot be put back together the way they were before. The beauty is that not only is this okay, it is freeing and incredible. It is a gift from the Universe, an opportunity to live a more expanded, intentional, and impactful life.

I started getting really curious about all forms of trauma healing. I got curious about addiction and the mental deterioration that a person goes through when they have one untreated relapse after another, after another, after another. I educated myself on how someone with Romeo's severe addiction and mental health issues could end up doing what he did. I got curious about why I stayed in the relationship as long as I did. I started feeling all the feelings. I sat with them until the point that I could integrate them into my reality. I deeply analyzed what my relationship was really like with Romeo all those years compared to the delusional version my mind created to deal with the pain and fear. I literally forced myself out of my comfort zone and challenged myself to feel everything about all those years with him and to see them for exactly what they were.

One of the most useful things I did was get a copy of all of my therapy records. I read every word from every therapy session. It was a very surreal experience to see how I described our relationship and all the things that happened. I was surprised at how deep in denial I was about what happened to me throughout the relationship. I was still justifying his behavior and never viewed myself as a victim. I also forced myself to obtain the police and hospital records. Going through this process was eye-opening in many ways, and it was critical in forcing me to acknowledge the reality of all that I went through. I remember when I got to the point of getting very angry with myself anytime I started having happy memories of him because the other part of me believed that he did not deserve any kind, loving memories. Neither part was wrong. I started grabbing a piece of paper every time I caught myself thinking about him or missing him. I would write down the actual thought I was having on one side of the paper, and then on the other side I would write out what Romeo was really like. Or if I had feelings of still loving him, I would try to write a list of all the wonderful things he did for me. That list was short, really short, when I took an honest inventory of how he treated me over the years. Even his proposal of marriage was half-assed and without any real effort, sincerity, or excitement about spending the rest of his life with me. The truth was Romeo was tired of his daughters and mom asking him when he was finally going to put a ring on my finger, so he just did it to shut them up and pacify me. There is tremendous healing power in the practice of regularly taking this fact vs. fiction inventory. You will eventually begin to see the person and the relationship for what it was, and then the deep healing can begin. This is a hard process to go through, and I had to learn to be kind to myself and not beat myself up for what I allowed and settled for.

I then started taking action to start releasing all the pain and toxicity from my body. I read books on trauma healing and addiction. I started writing, I started running, I started a yoga practice, I acknowledged my PTSD triggers, I did energy healing work, I spent every moment I could in nature, and I learned to love myself and find my identity again.

When a woman's safety and security is ripped away from her in the vulgar way that mine was in that hotel room, you have to learn to be a woman all over again. Period. The beauty in this is that you get to decide who that woman is going to be. I will go into further detail on how I rebuilt my entire life from the inside out in the next two chapters, but I wanted to dedicate this chapter to really focusing on the experiences I went through in healing the traumas from my relationship with Romeo. Acknowledging and healing these traumas provided me with the necessary foundation from which I could then build. If you are willing to do the work, you can authentically rise up and reincarnate from the fragments of your broken pieces.

As I was in the midst of writing this book, I took a self-defense course. I expected to walk away from this experience with proof that I had come as close to being "completely" healed from my trauma as one could possibly be. I had become a person who did not have any serious residual side effects from what happened other than that there were always going to be certain obvious triggers, but I knew those triggers and had equipped myself with the tools to effectively deal with them. What I walked away from this self-defense course with was confirmation that my initial hypothesis about trauma healing was true: There is no such thing as ever fully healing, as in, "Congrats. You passed, you're done, and it is all over and behind you."

The self-defense class started with the instructor giving a brief overview of the format and somewhat of a disclaimer that some people experience triggers during this course. I heard what she said but was not worried. I was bulletproof in my healing. I had done it the "right" way the second time through. Plus, this class was geared more toward a potential threat of sexual assault or an attack from a stranger. This was not the fact and circumstances of what I had gone through, so no worries.

We jumped into the training. The first exercise was to do some role-playing. An off-duty police officer came into the room dressed up as a creepy man wearing a mask. I was selected to go first. We were not told what to expect or what we were supposed to really do, but I was ready for anything. The guy started approaching me, getting up in my face. I looked him in the eyes and told him to back up and leave me alone. I didn't turn my back to him and kept moving so he would have to keep moving. I was visualizing a scenario where that could happen in real life, so I started waving my hands up in the air and raising my voice a little, saying I needed help, like I would do if that were actually happening. I looked over at the instructor, who gave me the cue to amp it up.

"Yell out for help," the instructor told me.

So, I did. "Help!" I screamed.

The moment I started really screaming for help, I had a full-on PTSD attack. The single worst one I had ever experienced. I could not catch my breath, suddenly started crying hysterically, and lost connection to the reality in the room.

I was literally in shock. I kept running through the role-play scenario in my mind to determine what triggered me, and not only triggered me but triggered me to the point of having a panic attack and completely breaking down. It happened when I started screaming for help. The vibration and tone of me raising my voice to a certain level triggered emotional trauma that was still trapped in my body. All I wanted to do was run out of that room and go home and curl up with my dog on the couch.

I spent the next 30 minutes contemplating my exit strategy. I really do not even know what was going on in that room. Leaving was complicated. I knew the instructor, and a friend and her daughter were in the class. I did not want to walk out and then have to explain myself later. Another complicating factor was that there was a 14-year-old girl taking the class with her mother. Watching all of us go through our role-play exercises triggered her, and she was crying hysterically. I asked her mom if she was crying because she had experienced trauma, and her mom said she had. Great, how the fuck could I let this 14-year-old girl see me leave when she was staying? I stayed, but I was not present. I could not concentrate. I felt anger building inside of me.

After class, the instructor asked me to give a brief interview about my experience. I don't remember what questions were asked or what I said other than I manically rambled on about having been through trauma and an abusive relationship. By the time class was finally over and I got home, I was in tears again. I was fucking pissed—back to being pissed at Romeo, at myself, and at the world. *How in the hell is it even in the realm of possibility after all the hard work that I had done on myself that I could react like that? What the actual fuck is the point of working that hard if after all that work, I could have a breakdown like that?*

I numbed out to some stupid TV show and a game on my phone because I did not want to process or think about what happened. I fell asleep with tears in my eyes. I woke up still feeling angry and decided that I needed to go running in the woods and spend some time alone with myself to understand what happened. I came back home feeling much better and knew that I needed to include this experience in the book. It happened for a very important reason, and this was to remind me that everything I had done to this point was not without purpose. What I experienced during that class was something for which I have immense gratitude for experiencing.

It provided beautiful insight into the fact that I am always going to need to be mindful of the fact that I have trauma stored in my body, and there most likely will be something else that will trigger a PTSD attack, and that is okay. It is not a sign of weakness; there is nothing that I need to be angry about. It is the reality of my life, and I will embrace it and hold it dear to my heart. I am not fragile. I am strong and resilient and 100% responsible for how I handle triggers when they occur. It is through the broken pieces that light may come in. The only way to truly heal is to let light in, and the only way to let the light in is through the expansion found in the beautiful, fragmented pieces buried in the depths of our souls.

I gave myself permission to feel everything, practice self-love, kindness, acceptance, compassion, and curiosity—all of which are the true secrets to healing from any trauma. While you will never go back to the person you were before the trauma, you absolutely can learn to live a full and amazing life while walking alongside the residual side effects of trauma. It is not through healing that you will love yourself. It is through loving yourself that you will heal.

The first time through healing, I covered every inch of my body in brightly colored tattoos to ease the blackness I felt inside and convinced myself that I was badass. I clawed my way through life trying to prove to everyone, including myself, that I was not a weak, broken victim. I now exist with the complete acceptance that I will always have latent triggers ready to spring into action. I didn't need to pretend to be a badass. I needed to become a physically, mentally, and spiritually expansive person to create the required space to live in peace alongside the pieces.

I have learned to face all my own demons.

I have learned to live in reality and see people and experiences for exactly what they are, including every aspect of my relationship with Romeo. I have learned to tell the truth and stop hiding in the protective shadows of what happened to me.

I have learned forgiveness.

I have learned compassion.

I have learned grace.

I have learned curiosity.

I have softened my identity and learned to embrace deep, authentic vulnerability. I have learned to become bendable but not breakable. I have learned that while addiction is not an excuse for why someone does something bad, it is an explanation as to why they do bad things, and those are two *very* different concepts. I found my passion and purpose in life. I have slowed down, learned to get to know myself for who I am now, and meet my own needs. I have accepted that I am a work in progress and will forever be one and that I heal myself deeper every time I own my story and share it with another soul. My goal is to no longer strive to reach a perceived place of being "healed" from my trauma. Rather, my goal is to softly lean into living as free as possible from the effects of my trauma. By freedom, I do not mean carefree. I mean free as in having a choice in how I view the things that happened to me and more importantly how I am going to grow from my trauma.

These words are written from the beautiful scars I earned through deep healing, not the wounds of all the things that happened to me. I pray you can learn from my words, as they are raw and authentic and written with the deep intention of helping people understand what it is genuinely like to love an addict and that some relationships cannot be saved. Some people are dangerous to be around, and you cannot risk losing your life trying to save someone else. Trauma forces us to close our hearts and armor up; healing teaches us to open our hearts and boundary up. You have to love yourself more than you love someone else, and honor the boundaries of a safe and healthy relationship.

What happened that night in the hotel, the hollow look in his eyes, the eerie words he spoke, the countless tears he shed, and my belief that I was going to die will haunt the outskirts of my mind forever. But from my near-death experience, I learned to be honest, to be brave, and to be absolutely fucking relentless in the pursuit of peace and happiness, and so can you.

CHAPTER 7

ADDICTION

I learned more about addiction from Romeo than I ever thought possible—things I wish I would not have learned. However, of all the experiences and personal information that I have shared here, I never would have imagined that this chapter about addiction would turn out to be the most challenging for me to write, but in a way that may surprise you. If I am being completely honest, it is what put finalizing this book on hold for several months. I could not in good faith proceed with finalizing it until I had done the work to be able to write this chapter with the ending my soul knew it needed. This chapter required of me an even deeper level of honesty and vulnerability: I had a problem. I was a binge drinker.

This problem was mine to fully own and did not arise because of any single thing or any one experience or because of anyone else. My being a binge drinker was not Romeo's fault. It has existed my entire adult life. Much like Romeo, my vice gripping approach to managing my use of alcohol was not successful. I had to do a lot of work to maintain long-term sobriety and acquire some important tools along the way.

I have surprised myself many times over the past few years and, more importantly, while journeying through my own healing process. My current sober lifestyle is the greatest surprise and gift of all. While at the onset of making the decision to write openly about my relationship with Romeo, the intent was to share the details of the things I experienced and the invaluable lessons that I learned so that I could help others heal with more ease and success than I did in my early attempts. What I did not expect was that this soul-searching to make peace with what had happened with Romeo would awaken within me the openness to approach all aspects of my own life with the same curiosity that I used to try to understand Romeo's drug addiction.

In experiencing firsthand the darkness and demons of addiction and loving an addict, I had this nagging thought in the back of my mind that kept echoing through my soul. I knew I had an unhealthy relationship with alcohol that I needed to take a serious look at. There were countless times that I could not control my drinking. I broke every boundary I set for myself. I had severe physical and emotional side effects each time I drank. The truth is that I have used and abused alcohol my whole life, just in very selective ways. While I have never been chemically dependent, the way Romeo was to meth and heroin, it did not mean that I did not experience many periods of time where I had a genuine problem with alcohol. Being a cute party girl or an occasional binge drinker or someone who only drinks when out with other people does not mean that you do not have an unhealthy relationship with alcohol. Read that last sentence one more time. It was true for me and could be true for you too.

Also weighing heavily on my heart was the guilt of how unauthentic I was to be exploring the subjects of addiction and healing with the goal of helping other people if I couldn't be honest with myself about my own drinking habits and how they were holding me back from living my best life. In the first year of moving to Fargo, I did not drink at all. It was not an intentional decision that I made. I was just so broken and fragile that it took everything I had to just go to work, the gym, and therapy. I had no interest in making friends or living outside that safety bubble I needed to survive. However, as time went on and I began healing, I also started making friends, dating, and socially drinking again. What I immediately noticed was that my body could no longer handle any amount of alcohol without severe emotional reactions either during or immediately after consuming it. I would feel a panic attack coming on as soon as the alcohol hit my system, so I drank more in hopes I would numb the panic attack and the racing thoughts that accompanied it. I also became extremely emotional and would start crying, which is very out of character for me. What I now know is that someone with trauma-induced PTSD should not consume alcohol. This angered me at the time. I remember having thoughts of being so angry at Romeo. Because of him and the things that happened, I could not even drink with my friends?

So, in August of 2019, I started getting really curious about alcohol, not only my use of it but alcohol itself. I read a fantastic book by Annie Grace called "The Alcohol Experiment." This experiment provides a practical guide to giving up alcohol for 30 days. Each day contains a lesson about alcohol with an emphasis on what happens in the brain and body when you consume it. You also keep a journal on what you are experiencing physically and mentally as you go through the 30 days. The first time through the book, I did the experiment half-assed. I read all the chapters and did some of the exercises, but I was resistant to a lot of it. What it did do was start explaining some things, like why ever since my trauma with Romeo, my body was not processing alcohol the same way it used to process it. And why I was waking up in the middle of the night with severe panic attacks even if my drinking had simply been a couple of beers at Happy Hour. After reading this book, a single flower seed had been planted in my soul to seek sober living.

During this same time, I was also getting curious about what I could do to make myself feel as healthy as possible. You see, I prepared for sharing my relationship with Romeo like a marathon runner prepares for their first marathon. For me to vulnerably share my experiences with the depth and quality that I was being called upon by the Universe to produce, I knew that I needed to be the healthiest person that I could be emotionally, spiritually, and physically. I knew alcohol did not feel good in my body as I was drinking my first drink. I also knew that despite how healthy I was eating, much of the food I was consuming also did not feel good in my body. I often felt bloated, my entire body was itchy, I had headaches every day, and my energy level was very low.

I decided to find a naturopathic doctor and undergo food allergy testing. The test produced a sheet of paper that showed 300+ foods and ingredients that I had an allergy or sensitivity to and then ranked them based on how highly sensitive I was to them. My eyes were instantly drawn to the fact that all the ingredients in a beer (my drink of choice) were on this list. My automatic response to my doctor was, "You mean I can't fucking drink beer anymore?"

The next morning, I took out the list again and was overwhelmed with emotion. Why was I not more concerned about all the food that I was sensitive to and would no longer be able to eat? Should I not have been more worried about the fact that I could not eat eggs, cheese, yogurt, or whey—foods I was consuming every day—than be worried about the beer or trying to figure out what I could drink instead of beer? I was saddened and a bit taken aback by my anger toward the thought of having to give up beer but not my favorite foods. I decided to re-do the Alcohol Experiment again. It was relatively easy this time around, and I completed 30 days sober AF (sober as fuck). Annie Grace refers to "AF" as being "alcohol free," but like everything in my life, I need to put my own spin on it to make it resonate in my soul, so I refer to it as being sober AF. There were now many flower seeds planted in my soul about living a sober life, and a few were just starting to grow solid roots.

In November of 2019, I had an office employee party on the calendar and dinner out with my girlfriends. I suddenly became consumed with how I was going to make it through those two events without alcohol. At that point, my body was feeling healthier than it had in 10 years. I began thinking that it may be easier to go and just have one drink like I had been easily able to do many times in life. But that bothered me because my heart and soul were really committed to remaining sober AF. Girl's night came first. The whole day was consumed with what I was going to do about drinking that night. I thought long and hard about not going, but really wanted to see my friends. Why was I still so consumed with alcohol? I left the house with the promise to myself that I would order a glass of water and nothing else. However, the moment I sat down at the table and looked at my friends with their wine, I thought, *Fuck it. I will just have one glass of wine with everybody.* I actually hate wine with a passion, but it was just easier than explaining to my friends why I was suddenly not drinking. I chose wine because I did not like it, so I assumed I would only be able to drink one. Well, one glass turned to three. I woke up at 4:00 a.m. the following morning sick and having a severe panic attack. I was pissed that I drank. I was pissed I wasted money on something I hated the taste of. I was pissed about how physically sick I was. All of this drama, and I fucking hate wine. Back to the 30-day experiment—round three.

Later that month, I had a huge office employee appreciation party on the calendar. This was a big event. I chaired the committee that was organizing the event, and I was being recognized for my achievements for the year. I was excited. But as the time drew nearer, so did the obsessive thoughts about alcohol. If I couldn't remain completely AF with a simple dinner with my girlfriends, how in the hell was I going to survive my office party? So, I simply did not go; truth is, I faked being sick. I was a successful 48-year-old lawyer who chaired the committee that organized the event, and I called in sick because of alcohol. I shook off the guilt of that and focused on the fact I was remaining sober and feeling great. Looked like I had it all figured out. I would just avoid any and all social encounters for the rest of my life. ...Sigh.

Early December rolled around, and I hit a phase of really missing bars. I missed simply enjoying a beer and engaging in a conversation with someone I did not know or enjoying a football game with other professional sports enthusiasts. I just fucking missed bars. Then that shady little part of my brain remembered that there was a chapter in the Alcohol Experiment that said (well, sort of said) that it is okay to experiment with consuming a few drinks, but you must make the conscious decision to drink ahead of time, plan out your rules around it, and either take notes or record yourself while drinking so that you can learn from the experiment (how do you feel, what thoughts are you having, are you sticking to the boundaries you set, etc.). The key here is that you consciously decide in advance that you are going to drink, what you are going to drink, how much you are going to drink, and that you take the time to analyze the experience. (This is completely different from the wine I drank in November because I did not intentionally plan to drink anything that night.)

I ended this intentional drinking experiment, drunk scribbling on a bar napkin about how I broke all my boundaries, felt like shit, did not even like the taste of beer anymore, didn't want to be drinking any more than the one beer I had planned on drinking, yet ordered another one anyway. I woke up the next day, looked at the scribblings on the ratty bar napkin, and said, "I am fucking done." I remained sober AF for the next 17 months until July 2020. I lived my absolute best life during that time. Those seeds that had been planted had not only grown roots, but they had bloomed into brightly colored flowers deep in the core of my soul.

One day in July 2020, I had just completed a 10-mile hike and decided to stop for lunch at a cute patio bar in a small town that I was traveling through. A thought popped into my head that said, "I think that I have been sober long enough now that I am healed from my drinking problems." The parking lot was full of motorcycles, and everyone was enjoying the beautifully sunny day and the views of the lake. I made a conscious decision to order a bloody mary— one of few alcoholic drinks that I truly enjoy the taste of. I slowly drank it, savoring the taste, feeling the alcohol move through my veins as it relaxed my body, enjoying the atmosphere around me and all that I was proud of in my life. I then ordered lunch and was on my way. I had no interest in ordering another one, but I did have some guilt over the fact that I was no longer "sober AF" by societal standards since I had one drink. That drink caused no triggers, no desires to drink the next day or thoughts that I could go back to drinking socially. It was what it was: a single drink on a beautiful summer day. I thought I finally had made peace with alcohol. I would live my best life being mostly sober. I was good with that. Problem solved. I had a total of maybe three or four drinks until April of 2021. With each of those drinks, one of those brightly colored flowers in my soul died.

In April of 2021, I took myself to Sedona for my 50th birthday. I went alone as I love solo travel adventures. The first night, I went to a beautiful patio bar overlooking the mountains. The sun was just starting to set. The waitress told me the drink special was a Sedona prickly pear mule. I wanted to try it. I loved it. I enjoyed the drink, my first Sedona sunset, and one of the best meals I have ever had.

Two days later, it was my birthday. I got up early and went on a long hike and then came back to town for breakfast. I was visiting with the waiter, and when he found out I was celebrating my 50th birthday, he said he had something special for me. He brought out a mimosa in a beautiful etched glass and a little bouquet of beautiful, fresh flowers. I love mimosas. I enjoyed every sip of that mimosa. He came back and asked if I wanted another, and I said, "No, just a coffee," without giving it much thought. The next morning, I got up early and drove to Phoenix for a sunrise hot air balloon ride. After the ride, the organization brought out a table and started making free mimosas. I had one and visited with the people that I had met, and we talked about how amazing the hot air balloon ride was. Someone handed me another one, and I drank it without really thinking. This time, I could feel the effects of those two drinks in my body. I honestly don't know what happened in my brain (upon reflection, this sounds exactly like what an addict says), but I immediately Googled "bars near me" and found a beautiful outdoor restaurant and had three more mimosas with breakfast. I was too embarrassed to order any more with the waitress at my table, so I closed out my tab and stopped at the bar of the same restaurant and ordered one more while I waited for my Uber to take me to the airport. I immediately found the first bar and ordered a beer. I took one sip, and I was sick. It tasted gross. It was noon, and I was fucking drunk. I felt like shit. I was in tears and broke out into a full panic attack. I could no longer by any creative definition say I was still "mostly sober." I have spent a lot of time thinking about what happened. How did it happen? How did I let it happen? Why did it happen? Was it because of the type of alcohol or because I drank on an empty stomach? I have no answers. It is truly like I did not have any rational explanation for what happened, and I still do not. Is that what happened to Romeo when he slipped into a relapse? I do know that I absolutely did not make a conscious choice to have any more than that first mimosa. It happened before I could consciously process that it was happening. I didn't say, "Oh, it's my birthday," or, "I am on vacation, so it's okay to drink to the point of getting drunk." It just fucking happened. I felt shame over the lack of conscious control I experienced. I was scared. I was painfully disappointed. To this very day, I still feel confused about what happened in my body and my mind between that one mimosa and being drunk in the airport a few hours later. All of this did allow me to deeply reflect on Romeo's addiction—all the times I looked at him with complete frustration and mistrust when he told me he did not know how he ended up using drugs again, that he did not mean for it to happen, and that he did not want to be like that.

This experience left me unsure of exactly what I needed to do next but with the knowing I needed to do something. Thus, I embarked on the next level of my winding journey to sober living. You see, a part of my mind was still holding on to those few times that I could have a drink or two and stop, rather than focusing on the drunken mess I was at the Phoenix airport. I am a social drinker and have always been a social drinker. By this, I mean the only time I drink is when I am out having fun. I have never been one to have alcohol in my home. It was just something that did not interest me. It was also something that kept my drinking problem hidden, or at least in my mind hidden. I can't possibly be an alcoholic or problem drinker if I only drink when I am out doing something, right? Wrong. But that took me a little while longer to accept into my reality.

While what happened in Phoenix scared me, I still convinced myself that a night out with the girls a few times a year was fine. No real consequences, except for the fact that it would take over a week for my body to regulate itself after one of those "harmless" nights out. And that week was pure hell. My PTSD controlled my thoughts and body until I could do enough things to bring myself back to "normal." A part of me knew the fun nights out were not worth what I experienced afterward. The problem was I had another part of me having fun again, having girlfriends again, and living life like I used to before everything happened with Romeo. On one shoulder sat a voice saying, "You know you need to go back to sober living." On the other shoulder sat a slightly louder voice saying, "You have been through so much. You deserve to live life the way you want, and everyone drinks, so why should you not be able to do the exact same thing?" Over the next few months, I picked the louder voice and had a few fun nights out with my girlfriends. The result was always the same. I drank way too much, and my body and mental health paid the price. I regretted it, but eventually after enough time passed, I did it again.

So what if I drank once a month or every two months? That was a lot less than most people I knew, and it is not like what happened in Phoenix had happened again. Of the handful of times I drank between April 2021 and December 2021, I had consciously made the choice to do so, unlike the Phoenix situation. It was, therefore, okay that I occasionally drank.

New Year's Eve 2021 was upon me. I had planned to go out of town with my dog on a road trip, which is how I spent every New Year's Eve since I had moved to Fargo. I loved the energy of waking up on New Year's Day somewhere far from home. However, the weather didn't cooperate, and I was stuck in town. I was torn between just staying home or going out with my besties. I went against what my inner voice (the wise one, the one you should *always* listen to) said, which was to stay home. But that sounded depressing, so I decided to go out. However, I was only going to go out for a little while and only have two beers with dinner and then go home, as I had a fun day planned for New Year's and wanted to wake up feeling good. That did not happen. Somewhere between that first beer and 2:00 a.m., the Phoenix situation repeated itself. Those once beautiful, brightly colored flowers in my soul had all died by then. Why wouldn't they? I had been watering them with poison for months. I felt the heavy weight of the dead, black petals in every corner of my soul. I knew what I needed to do.

Keep in mind that up until that point, I had never sought out any support for my drinking other than reading a book or two, primarily because I didn't really believe that I had a problem that I could not "fix" on my own. I just had not tried hard enough. I had made some poor choices, but I had the ability to make better choices. As these thoughts were circulating in my mind, I could not help but remember the thousands of times Romeo had said those exact words to me. I recall telling him every time that while his addiction was not his fault, he needed help and support just like anyone else in his shoes would. How could he not see that he needed help and that he needed complete abstinence from drugs and alcohol? Yet, I couldn't get myself to admit that I, just like Romeo, was not going to be able to stay sober long-term by vice gripping.

The truth was I did not want to drink because I did not like how I felt when I did or the next day. Yet,

I could not force myself to completely refrain. I had the same cognitive dissonance with my alcohol use as I did with severing my addiction to Romeo: *I don't want to do this, but I can't stop doing this.* Resolving this cognitive dissonance is the fundamental key to overcoming any addiction. If you do not want to be doing something, but cannot stop doing it, you have a problem. Period. Being defiant is in my nature, and I hate rules. I hate being "told" that I can or cannot do something. I also did not want to lose the friendship with my girlfriends or miss out on fun times because I was not drinking. It was no wonder I had not been able to stop on my own with no support and no tools to fall back on when I wanted to drink or found myself in situations where alcohol was unexpectedly present. What I needed to do was admit deep within my soul that I needed to permanently remove alcohol from my life, and I wasn't going to be able to do that alone.

So, I got busy. I re-read "The Alcohol Experiment" and did another 30-day challenge. This time, I had the benefit of all the data I had collected from all my attempts at limiting my drinking or vice gripping my abstinence over the past two years. It was different this time. I now accepted myself as someone with a drinking problem and, more importantly, someone who needed to permanently remove alcohol from her life. I worked so hard at healing from my traumas with Romeo that I do not want to harm my body, mind, or soul any longer with alcohol. I reconnected with some sober girlfriends and started getting together with them for support. I sought out a sponsor, and it took a few to find one that was a good match for what I needed from a sponsor. I read other books on alcohol recovery. I experimented with a couple of types of recovery meetings in an attempt to find something that resonated with my soul. While I continue to gain wisdom and loving support for my sobriety from a weekly Women's AA meeting, there are parts about AA that I personally struggle to agree with and things I feel are missing, especially as a woman. So, I am in the process of creating my own sober living support group to fill in those missing pieces. If I am feeling like this, so are other women. The interrelationship between women who struggle with addiction, eating disorders, and domestic violence is deeply woven together. Since I have a lifetime of experience with all three issues, I might as well put all that knowledge to good use. I fully owned and identified to the world that I was choosing to live a sober AF lifestyle. Through the process of doing these things and once again feeling the mental and physical benefits of not having alcohol in my body, I made the peaceful, intentional decision to remain sober AF until the end of my days. In those moments of releasing the shame around my problem drinking, I felt so empowered. Just like the empowerment I felt when I learned to release the shame of allowing myself to stay in a dangerous relationship that almost cost me my life.

Like everything in life, sobriety is not a destination you arrive at but rather an ongoing journey that requires awareness, honesty, and, most of all, support. What I need today to remain sober may not be the same a month from now or six months from now. But with the wholehearted decision to remain sober AF came an enormous amount of freedom and peace. I no longer analyze and reanalyze the facts to determine if I really have a problem with alcohol or spend countless hours planning what my drinking boundaries need to be now. It is easy. I will not drink, and I will do whatever is necessary to maintain my sobriety. Asking for help when needed is not a sign of weakness but rather a badass act of strength. I have gone through my entire life never asking anyone for help with anything. If someone offered it to me, I refused it because somewhere deep inside there was a part of me that didn't think I deserved help. I grew up believing love and support had to be earned. I know better now. When you know better, you do better.

Learning to live without alcohol is not without challenges. The difference now is that I have made peace with my decision and finally resolved that cognitive dissonance. I accepted into my reality the deep all-knowing that on-going support is a requisite for my long-term sobriety. Most importantly, I am now in alignment with my soul and how I genuinely want to live my life. As I am reviewing this manuscript one final time, I have now been sober AF for almost a year. And that flower garden in my soul is blooming once again, more radiantly colored than before, deeply rooted, nourished daily, and carefully protected. My greatest act of healing from trauma is living a sober life.

CHAPTER 8

CREATING AN EXTRAORDINARY LIFE FROM THE INSIDE OUT

I vividly recall that fall of 2015, being curled up in a lifeless ball on the floor of the home I had been sharing with Romeo. I had been wearing the same clothes for going on four days, crying, fragile, unemployed, in debt, and scared. Nothing had changed, yet everything had changed. When Romeo went on the run, he took nothing with him, not even a single piece of clothing. The smell of his cologne still lingered in the air, and his energy haunted every corner of every room in that house. I was paralyzed by life. Knowing there were a hundred things that I needed to do, but unable to so much as take a shower, let alone begin to tackle the world, left me on the verge of suicide. *How did I get here, and what in the fuck do I do now?* Lying next to me was the denial letter from my unemployment, a phone full of messages from Romeo, a sheriff's car once again parked outside, and the echo of the voice of my landlord tenderly explaining that he was going to have to start looking for a new tenant if I could not get caught up on rent by the end of the week.

Today, though, is a different story. I awoke to the sunrise illuminating the sky over my beautiful apartment, my dog, Maicy, snuggled up next to me, planning the details of my upcoming solo travel adventure to Honduras. I continue to be a successful corporate attorney for one of the world's largest technology companies. I feel extremely grateful for every little thing I have. In a way, one can only be truly grateful for having first fallen so far down the black hole of despair you had to crawl your way back up into the light. So much has changed over the last few years that it sometimes seems hard to believe. The residual effects are still there, but I have now accepted that and move through life knowing that there is nothing that I cannot overcome and not only overcome but conquer.

In between who I was six years and who I am today was a wild ride of balancing what had happened with continuously upleveling to where I wanted to go next. In those early fragile days, I was alone, more alone than I thought was possible, riddled with shame and disappointment in myself, yet somewhere deep inside was still a flicker of hope in the single remaining fragment of my soul that had not been shattered. There is a place in everyone's soul where you have never been wounded. It is in this place that we find who we really are. We get so busy with how to heal and what we need to do that we overlook the very first step: connecting back to our soul, for it is from within our soul that the healing process begins. We have to shed all the armor that the trauma required us to wear for protection, or no amount of talk therapy or any book or mediation or support group is going to truly work. You need to stop focusing on this perceived notion that there is some magic formula to healing, because there is not. It is a soul journey, just as overcoming addiction is a soul journey. And you have to start from within to begin. You need to release the shame, blame, and anger over the things you cannot control and treat your soul with compassion and curiosity. You also need to release all the false identities that surfaced after that armor went on. The victim identity, the martyr, the badass, tough girl, or whatever it may be for you. You have to create space to heal and sit in the shit while simultaneously taking a small step forward into the journey of extraordinary living after trauma. Become an adventurer of your own soul.

For me, I began to focus on those moments in that hotel room when I did not think I was going to live, and I remembered that what saddened me the most were all the undone things in my life that were flashing before me, thinking that my life was going to end before I had fully lived and experienced all that was intended for me. I slowly stopped feeling sorry for myself and started feeling gratitude for being alive. I mean, most people will obviously say they are grateful for being alive, but not because they had tip-toed up to death's door, knocked, but then by miracles that cannot be explained, got to walk away. I started there. As many times a day that I could, I started there in that feeling place of gratitude. I started listening to music that moved my soul. After a few days of reveling in this space of gratitude and music, I wrote out on the back of one of my many overdue bills a list of what I needed to do, and slowly, item by item, day by day, I started crossing things off that list. With every item I checked off, I built momentum. I generated within me a light that I didn't know was still there. It was as if a spark had been lit within that tiny, still alive part of my soul. With each small task I managed to accomplish, that spark grew bigger within me.

Within a month, I had secured a new job, sold everything I could, found an apartment, and moved to Moorhead, Minnesota. Once I moved, I started a new list. I got a dog for emotional support, joined a gym, found a trauma therapist, and made the really difficult decision to file Chapter 13 Bankruptcy, which allowed me five years to pay off the overwhelming amount of debt Romeo had caused me to incur. Once I completed one list, I moved on to a new list. This is upleveling. I am still doing this same practice today. There is always an open list that I am working from. When you take one step toward the Universe, the Universe takes 10 steps toward you. The key here is that YOU need to take that first gentle baby step forward.

In addition to gratitude and taking action, I began to live my best life independent of anyone else. One of the main reasons I ended up finding myself in a toxic relationship was because I was not filling the voids in my life. I allowed space for someone else to come in and do that for me and in very destructive ways. I have spent the last four years listening to what my heart, soul, mind, and body need and then finding healthy ways to give myself what I need. I have put nothing on hold in my life that I want to do because of fear or because I do not have someone to hold my hand along the way. I have also built a tribe of soul family that brings me to tears with gratitude. I sought out those people I wanted in my life and became the person I needed to become so that the Universe could connect us. I have learned to embrace my restless soul rather than try to hide it. As a result, I have been ticking off bucket list adventures that make me feel alive like I have never been before. I have solo traveled to Peru and trekked Machu Picchu, gone skydiving, completed six spartan races, road-tripped my way across five US states, and spent two weeks driving a Happy Camper around the entire country of Iceland.

I often get asked if I fear that I could once again find myself in a relationship with another Romeo. I can say with absolute certainty that it will never happen again. I have put as much, if not more, effort into ensuring that it does not happen than I did in obtaining my law degree and 24 successful years of being an attorney. I built a healthy, solid foundation around my life. I have healed my childhood wounds and filled those other empty voids that left me vulnerable to someone like Romeo coming in. I removed the shame that held me back from recognizing my own self-worth. I started living a sober life with peace and honesty. This does not mean that I do not have to be vigilant about checking in with myself, what I am feeling, and what I need. It also does not mean that I do not have moments of vulnerability or take missteps—or a few rolls down a hill. That is human, and extraordinary living like this is not a destination; it is an endless journey of alchemy—learning, growing, and expanding into the next evolution of yourself.

As I look back over the course of my relationship with Romeo, I am struck by how obvious it was that he was a deeply troubled man. I collected his red flags and turned them into bouquets of roses and methodically placed them in beautiful, fragile vases for all to see, except for myself. I was blinded by love addiction, living in a complete state of dissociation, and had no ability to change from who I was to who I wanted to become. I lost myself, my boundaries, my identity, and my voice. I believed that I could somehow make him get help. Hear this loud and clear: No one is ever going to be able to make another person get clean and sober if that person does not want to get clean and sober. You cannot love them enough, mother them enough, or be a good enough person to make them get clean or sober. That is between the individual and their addiction. Period. There is a critically important line between sticking by someone and protecting your own well-being. I let Romeo not only cross that line, but I almost lost my life in the process of waiting for him to get the help he needed. I cannot stress this enough. I gave away my power to another human being to the extent that it almost cost me my life. Let that sink in. Never love someone to the point of losing yourself. That is not love; that is a delusion with a trauma bond anchor securely attached to it. You need to look inside of yourself to determine how and why you let that happen just like I painfully had to do. Supporting someone who is getting help is one thing; risking your own life for a person who has no rational ability to care for themselves, let alone you, is not acceptable. Learn from my mistakes. If a man hits you once, he will hit you again. If you are asking yourself if your relationship is unsafe, the unequivocal answer is yes. Leave. Let them heal themselves. Nothing that is truly meant for you will ever miss you in life. If love is meant to be, it will find its way to you. And by no definition does love include putting yourself in an unhealthy and dangerous situation. Never, and I repeat never, justify your scars just because you loved the person holding the knife.

I want to close with encouragement for your own soul journey. It starts with small steps and an unwavering commitment to do the work to heal. Learn from my mistakes. Put that foundation around your life that creates the environment needed to foster healing and recovery. Take a close look at your life, and identify any issues that may be getting in your way of living your best life, and deal with them. Love yourself as you are, but be willing to do the work to uplevel into the next best version of who you are truly capable of becoming, the version your soul is calling you to become. Your soul will not stop calling until you rise up from the ashes to reach your true soul purpose.

I believe that we all come into this world with a soul contract. It is our responsibility during the course of our life to fulfill that soul contract. Your soul is going to keep calling you to fulfill this contract. I now know that my soul contract is to be of service to those who have experienced domestic violence and addiction. A critical part of my soul contract was to be an abused woman and a woman who loved an addict. I am now going to move on to the next phase of fulfilling my soul contract.

I do not even recognize the fragile woman I was six years ago. I honor her for her strength, resilience, and sheer determination. I am relieved that I will never be her again because of the amount of work I have done to heal. While every day I set the intention to strive to be a little better version of myself than the day before, I am living the absolute best days of my life right now. I would never be as happy, healthy, and fulfilled as I am today had it not been for all that I learned from my relationship with Romeo. While this did not turn out to be a happily ever after love story between Romeo and I, it is a true love story of how a woman ended up madly falling in love with herself for the first time and reinventing her life from the foundation up. At some point, you must step out of that safe space you healed in and live your life to the fullest. That is where the real magic exists.

I will gracefully move forward spending the rest of my days helping other women do the same, and each of you hold within you the power to follow in my path. The most important journey in life is that of coming back home to who you really are. Let the pain and struggle move through you rather than allow it to continue happening to you over and over in your mind. My struggle is my greatest gift because it has forced me to become who I am today, and I could not be prouder of how that woman is showing up in the world today. It is through the struggle that the greatest transformations become possible. Make sure you lovingly give yourself the credit for gaining the strength to heal.

My trauma did not make me stronger. My trauma made me broken and weak. It gave me complex PTSD and dysregulated my entire nervous system. It gave me feelings and experiences that I never wanted. It left me to live alongside ghosts and haunting memories. My trauma literally almost killed me. I made myself strong by dragging myself inch by inch out of the blackness and into the light—a light that I now proudly carry in my soul for others to find their way back home to their soul. Let the legacy of domestic abuse survivors be a collective imprint on the world, one in which shame is replaced with bravery and silence is replaced with the voice of truth. In the moment that we own our story, we take back our power. It is only when you take complete responsibility for your life that you are able to discover how powerful you truly are. Own your story, and use it to empower the next woman to do the same.

Love and light from my soul to yours.

A FREE CHECKLIST

I have created a free checklist to help you determine if you or someone you love is in an unhealthy/ abusive relationship.

- Checklists serve as a powerful tool to identify concerning behaviors and safety risks.
- Checklists provide you with a way to acknowledge and assess unhealthy aspects of your relationship.
- Checklists are private and confidential.

Go to **www.loriabbott.pubsitepro.com** to pick up your free gift and to find out about my upcoming events!

Please email me with any questions or comments regarding *The Romeo & Juliet Delusion* at **ljabbott15@gmail.com.**

Made in the USA
Middletown, DE
27 April 2023

29520127R00088